Lone Wolf

Terry Gorger

Copyright © 2024 by Terry Gorger

All rights reserved.

No portion of this book may be reproduced in any form without written permission from the publisher or author, except as permitted by U.S. copyright law.

Contents

~~ONE~~	1
~~TWO~~	7
~~THREE~~	17
~~FOUR~~	26
~~FIVE~~	34
~~SIX~~	44
~~SEVEN~~	53
~~EIGHT~~	63
~~NINE~~	72
~~TEN~~	81
~~ELEVEN~~	88
~~TWELVE~~	95
~~THIRTEEN~~	104
~~FOURTEEN~~	111
~~FIFTEEN~~	119

~~SIXTEEN~~	126
~~SEVENTEEN~~	134
~~EIGHTEEN~~	143
~~NINETEEN~~	150
~~TWENTY~~	159
~~EPILOGUE~~	166

~~ONE~~

Welcome to chapter one my readers! Above is Fleura's wolf form, beautiful huh? I wrote this while listening to Howl by Florence and the Machine.~~~~~~
~~~~~~~~~~~~~~~

Fleura

This is not how I thought I'd be spending my night.

I push faster as the yelling gets closer, my paws pounding the dirt as I attempt to avoid the hunters behind me. I had shifted to go for my usual twilight run, and accidentally came into the sight of hunters.

Not just any hunters, but werewolf hunters. Humans who despise the Werewolf species and hunt us for sport, killing us for fun. Claiming that monsters like us shouldn't be allowed to live...like that makes slaughtering defenseless pups right.

I weave in and out of the trees, following the instincts of my wolf Aurora as we try to shake them off our tail. The sound of gunshots sending another burst of adrenaline through my exhausted body, I honestly don't know if I can keep running like this for much longer.

Searing pain rips through my shoulder, the silver bullet biting my skin and pulling a painful cry from my muzzle. I stumble at the pain, my pace slowing down even more. Even if it's just a graze, the silver is slowing down the healing process.

"Hit her again, she's slowin' down!"

One of the men yells out, and I limp-run as fast as possible. Just as I thought they were gonna catch me, the sound of a vicious growl echoes ferociously loud through the cold air, the screams and yells of terror making me hesitate. I stand and listen to the awful noises, a few stray gunshots firing as the sound of tearing flesh and the smell of blood invades my senses.

The last fired shot is followed by an almost simultaneous cry of pain, and despite my usually better judgment, I can't stop myself from going back to see what happened.

This is a bad idea...even if it is a werewolf that saved me, I have no idea who they are. For all I know they could be a hungry rouge cannibal who just happened to cross this way...and decided to eat the hunters.

What am I thinking?

As I slowly limp closer, another smell creeps through the air. And unlike the smell of death and blood, it is actually a pleasant smell...really pleasant.

Caramel and pecans...with a hint of brown sugar and vanilla.

Warm, alive...intoxicatingly sweet.

Looking over the carnage before me, my gaze falls onto the the one individual who looks out of place...the only one without clothes on.

The delicious aroma seems to be coming from him, and I unwittingly move closer. Curiosity quickly becomes panic when I notice the exit wound on his broad, tattooed back. He was shot... he's dying!

I press my muzzle against his shoulder and flip him over as gently as possible, and cry out in surprise. I had forgotten he wasn't wearing clothes for a moment, and nearly looked too far.

Pulling my thoughts back to the more important problem, I try to wake him from his sleeping state. Pressing my nose to his neck, gently pawing at his shoulders, whining and licking his face...no results.

I have to find a way to help him, he got shot while saving my life, I can't just leave him here to die. But I can't shift back right here, I'm too exposed this close to the regular trails.

Noticing one of the hunters had a tarp in his hand, no doubt to wrap me up in once I was dead, I yank it out of his grasp and spread it out as best as I can. Taking the handsome strangers wrist in my teeth as carefully as possible, I drag him onto the tarp so I can pull him to my home, making sure I keep my eyes above his shoulders the entire time.

I keep a constant ear out on his heartbeat as I pull him to my home, a small cabin in the woods, not wanting him to die before I could really help him. Making it home, I shift back and enter through the back door, pulling on some clothes of my own and grabbing a blanket to drape over the bleeding stranger.

Gripping under his arms, I drag him inside while he is still on the tarp, the old blanket draping over his lower half haphazardly. I lock the door and grab the first aid kit, deciding just to treat him on my tiny kitchen floor.

As my fingers brush over his chest, warm sparks erupt through my hand, making me jump back in surprise. It's like a static shock, except it didn't hurt....but felt really nice for some odd reason. I push it aside as I inspect his injuries, and thank the goddess the bullet passed through, which means I don't have to dig it out.

I pour peroxide over both sides of his wound, cleaning around them before covering it with gauze and wrapping around his stomach with the bandages to hold it in place. Goddess he is heavy, what does he eat? Cinderblocks?

Now that he is patched up, I take a moment to actually look him over. Shiny, black hair falls gently down past his shoulders, the long tendrils looking like they'd be soft to the touch. Dark stubble forms a slight shadow over his strong jaw, a dimple sitting in the dead center of his chin.

Barbed wire wraps around the thick bulge of his right bicep, a strange symbol in blue ink sitting in the center. A metal chain hangs from his neck, the design on the circular pendant one I don't really recognize...only that it's a pair of wolves. My eyes skim down his chest, lingering on the shield tattooed over his heart before continuing to his stomach, the well defined muscle evident even through the bandage, as well the tattoos inked onto the skin.

A vine of what appears to be roses curls around a sword on the right side of his stomach, while a tribal pattern follows the v-line just above where his pants would-

I snatch my eyes back upwards, a hot blush burning my cheeks. Why on earth am I checking out a stranger that's unconscious on my floor?

I stand up and think for minute. I can't just leave him on the floor now can I? The dilemma is does he go in the tiny guest room on the opposite side of the house, or to the couch that's only a few feet away...

Couch it is.

I begin pulling him again, the tingling spreading up my arms from the contact with his bare chest. I silently pray to the goddess that the blanket doesn't slip down any further, I've already been tested twice and nearly failed...a third time will actually give me a heart attack.

I hoist him onto the couch after multiple attempts, his humongous frame nearly squishing me from the weight. I pull the blanket up to his shoulders, not wanting any more temptations than I already had, and slide a pillow under his head. His steady breathing and relaxed expression a relief to my ears, and I get up to clean the mess in the kitchen...only to feel a stabbing pain in my shoulder. Darn it, I forgot about that.

I head to the kitchen and tend my own wound, the grazed skin burning at the touch. After rinsing it out with water and cleaning it with peroxide, I patch it up, taping the gauze over the damaged skin.

This is going to hurt for a while.

I sigh and clean up the mess on the floor, stuffing the bloody tarp in the metal drum outside to burn it later. I do not need an excuse for cops to come sniffing around, that would be far from helpful.

Heading back inside, I put the kit away and head back to the living room, staring at the stranger again.

There is a stranger in my house...a naked, handsome, werewolf stranger...he could be rabid for all I know and I brought him here. I know I couldn't have just left him to die, but bringing him here wasn't a good idea either...what do I do when he wakes up?

My thoughts whirl around inside my head as I pace, my feet moving as fast as my thoughts.

This is bad, really, really bad. He could be a psycho! I saw what he did to those hunters, what if he attacks me? I couldn't fight him off...not without getting hurt...

I stop in my tracks and stare at him again, even when he's sleeping you can tell he's powerful, it practically radiates of him. I can only guess though, I've never been part of a pack...I've never even met a pack affiliated wolf...

not personally anyway. I avoid them as much as possible, not wanting any chance of being mistaken for a rouge and killed for it.

~He's very powerful...he must be a high ranking pack member...very handsome too....~ Aurora whispers in my head, and I can't deny either of those things.

But it still doesn't make this a good idea.

~~TWO~~

A bove^^^ Fleura's eyes! Light blue and emerald green. Pretty huh?~~~~~~~~~~~~~~~~~~~~~~~~~~

Dakota

The first thing that hits me is the pain. A searing burn in my side that sends me growling, shifting uncomfortably.

Cracking my eyes open, I make the quick realization that instead of being outside where I'm supposed to be, I'm inside someone's house.

Trying to get up, the pain shoots through me again, and my hand goes towards the source of the discomfort, and I encounter a bandage wrapped around my stomach. Whoever's home I'm in, they fixed me up as well...

I carefully sit up, inhaling deeply as the action pulls the damaged muscle. The scent that hits the back of my throat startles me, the sweet aroma saturating everything around me and hanging heavy in the air.

Blueberries, bananas...maple syrup...it smells like blueberry banana pancakes......my favorite.

The fact that I smell another werewolf lets me know the scent isn't from food, but from the wolf themselves. A secondary scent of beef and vegetables makes my stomach rumble in hunger, but Zayev is more occupied with the other wolf...and so am I.

~smells like mate...go to them...~ He growls lowly, impatiently pacing around in my head.

~You and I both know that can't be right, our mate rejected us.~

A sharp pain stings in my chest, and I try to brush it off. I found my mate over a year ago, and she rejected us because I was a Gamma...and she'd rather have an Alpha. She rejected me because I wasn't ranked high enough for her standards.

Besides...that she wolf had a spicy scent...not at all like this one.

~our mate...I can tell. They are ours.~

As in...a second chance mate?

I groan as I pull up straight, the heavy quilt that's draped over my chest sliding down to reveal the bandage, a bit of blood leaking through it. I look around the room I'm in from my place on the couch, the wood paneled walls are dark, the cream colored carpet giving a rustic look. Wood furniture and a dark red recliner fill the small space, and besides the window there is only a clock on the wall. A lit, brick fireplace sits opposite of the couch, a large basket of firewood sitting in front of it.

I turn my attention back to the bandage, lifting the edge to try and see it. Bad idea. The action stings my skin, eliciting another growl.

"Fuck." I spit out irritably.

A light squeak comes from across the room, and I look up to see where it came from...and I'm met with an beautiful sight. Standing in the entrance is a young she-wolf, her wavy, ice blonde hair flowing down to her hips. The pale ivory skin of her face is flushed pink, making the the freckles that are sprinkled over her nose and across her cheekbones standout. Her soft, slightly rounded cheeks and plump lips make her look like a child rather than an adult...a real life cherub.

A lock of her blonde hair hides the right side of her face, leaving one eye covered. The uncovered eye is emerald in color, glittering brightly as she stares. Most of her short stature is hidden under a tan shawl, but her tiny hands play with her hair nervously under my gaze.

~mate...~ Zayev rumbles, and the slightest of growls reverberates in my chest.

She is truly beautiful.

"Y-you are awake..." Her soft voice barely audible, I strain my ears to hear her shy whispers. I make her nervous...that bothers me more than I expected.

"Who are you? What am I doing here?"

I try to ask in a normal voice, my usual gruff tone would probably only make her more timid. She shivers at the sound of my voice, and I can't tell if it's from fear...or something else.

"I am F-Fleura...you were hurt, so I brought you here..."

~Fleura...perfect...~

I suddenly recall the hunters I encountered as I was out on my nightly run, they were chasing after a wolf...hunting it...

"Hit her again, she's slowing down!"

"You are the wolf they were shooting at, aren't you?" Zayev growls in my head, not liking the fact she was in danger.

She nods, hesitantly stepping closer. I fight the urge to move directly in front of her, wanting to tangle my hands in her soft hair and trace over her lips...it would probably terrify her right now.

"Why did you bring me here?" I ponder out loud, considering she's this nervous around me, why would she go through all the trouble?

"You were shot with silver and you saved my life, I-I couldn't just let you die..."

So she brought me here, and mended my wounds...took care of me while I was healing. It dawns on me that she got shot too.

"But weren't you injured?"

She nods and brings a hand up to her right shoulder, no doubt where she was hit.

"It was j-just a graze, it's already healed."

Her gaze flickers towards my stomach, resting on the bandage before returning to my face. A faint smile curls my mouth at the action, and as much as I know the awful way this can end, I can't help but want to get close to her. Potential painful rejection be damned.

"You can come closer, little one, I won't bite." Not yet, and not in a way that'll hurt, anyway.

She turns from pink to red, carefully walking towards me. I can't stop the chuckle that her shy behavior brings, clearly she hasn't been in the company of male wolves very much...not that I'm complaining.

Her delicious scent becomes even more intense as she finally stands in front of the couch I'm on, sitting on the stool as she holds her hand just above my bandaged wound. Since it seems she's uncertain about touching me, I go to grab her hand, savoring the warm sparks for a split second before she jumps back in surprise.

"What-What is that?"

Her baffled expression is extremely genuine, which throws me off. Has she not heard of mates? She clearly knows the werewolf world, so how could she...unless...

I discretely inhale her scent again. The wolf is there, but the woodsy scent of a pack isn't...but neither is a rouge scent...is it possible she's a lone wolf? They're not common, but there are a few out there that were never born into a pack. Their usually called gypsy wolves, and they occasionally grow up like humans and have limited knowledge on packs and werewolves.

"Are you hurt?" I ask, inconspicuously probing.

"No-it just, felt strange...did you feel it too?"

"Yes, but it didn't hurt me either, you can check my wound now."

She bites her bottom lip, and I push back my instinct to kiss it. She takes a pair of scissors and carefully cuts the bandage away, revealing the blood stained gauze beneath, no doubt a product of my impatience. Her gentle touch on my skin takes away the pain as she redresses my wound, even when she poured peroxide on the irritated skin. She just spreads some ointment on the damaged areas before placing two large band-aids over them, which means the wounds have healed considerably.

She would make an excellent pack doctor, that is if she was part of a pack.

"Have you not been in a pack before?" I ask despite myself, and her head pops up at the question.

"No. But you are...right?"

"I am, though it's been over a year since I've been in contact with them." I admit.

"Why is that?" She asks, a small tilt of her head making her look adorable.

"I went on a search for my mate..."

"Did you find them?"

I sigh. "I did...but she rejected me..."

Her expression softens, a look of empathy in her gaze.

"I'm so sorry..."

"It's alright little one, it was a long time ago. She was just after rank anyway, and I wasn't high enough for her."

"You seem very powerful to me, she must of been completely oblivious."

I chuckle, me and Zayev both swelling with pride at the compliment. She's never been in the presence of an Alpha, or she would've been able to tell. But it doesn't take away from my pride that she thinks so highly of me.

"She wanted an Alpha, and nothing less would be good enough."

"You aren't an Alpha?"

"No my dear Fleura, I'm a Gamma, third in command."

"Oh...that's still impressive though, she must not have been smart enough to see it."

Whether she's aware of it or not, her honest praise makes me extremely happy.

"Do you have a mate Fleura?"

She shakes her head after a moment of hesitation, seeming confused as she does. I silently hope it's because she subconsciously knows I'm her mate, but is just not aware of the fact.

"I know that every wolf has one, and that they're like your other half...but I don't know much else."

I sigh in relief, thanking the goddess that she feels the mate bond, but just doesn't know what it is.

"I'm sorry. I'm rambling on and I don't even know your name."

Her shyness reappears once again, her soft blush making a quick return.

"My name is Dakota Jackson, but you can just call me Dakota."

"Alright...Dakota..."

I suppress another growl, enjoying how she says my name. She suddenly pops up from her seat, making me jump in surprise.

"Oh, my soup!"

She sprints towards what I assume is the kitchen, leaving me in the living room laughing. After a few minutes, my body reminds me I haven't moved in a couple days.

"Where is the bathroom?" I ask as I stand up, moving the quilt as I do.

"It's right down the--eeep!"

She had walked back into the living room just as I stood up, the quilt falling halfway to the floor revealing my lack of clothing. Her shocked little squeal cuts off what she was saying, and she whips back around with a red face.

"I'm sorry Fleura, I didn't mean to startle you."

She shakes her head furtively, and I bite back a chuckle.

"It's-it's okay...the bathroom is down the hall to the right..." She murmurs shyly before returning to the kitchen, no doubt still fire engine red. I turn in the direction she told me and make my way to the the small bathroom, me and Zayev a bit amused by her innocent reaction.

After relieving myself and washing my hands, I open the door to find a pair of sweatpants and boxers folded on the floor, they look brand new, and Fleura's scent is faint on the soft fabric. I duck back into the bathroom to put them on, the boxers a bit too tight while the sweatpants are a bit loose. She more than likely bought them for me, the sizes wrong because she didn't know what to get.

To be honest, I wouldn't mind walking around the house in just my birthday suit, I have no shame in my looks...but, this isn't my house, and even though the she wolf in it is my second chance mate, she has no idea that I'm all hers...so that'll have to wait until she's much more comfortable around me.

I exit the bathroom once more and make my way back through the living room before going to the tiny kitchen, seeing Fleura at the stove with her back turned to me. A large pot sits on the stove, the contents smelling delicious to my empty stomach, making it rumble noisily.

"Here you go..."

She turns slowly to hand me a bowl of what appears to be beef stew, with large chunks of beef, potatoes, carrots and small traces of onions in it. Her eyes avoid looking at me shyly, no doubt worried that I'm still undressed.

"Thank you for the clothes. And the food, it smells wonderful."

She looks up at me as I take the bowl from her, and the action draws attention to the covered side of her face. I carefully put the bowl down and reach for the lock of hair that hangs over her eye, her staring at me as she freezes. I push the lock behind her ear, the softness of the tendrils forgotten as I stare at the now exposed side of her face.

To be truthful, I don't know which is more shocking to me.

First, it's her eye itself. She has heterochromia. Her left eye is emerald green while her right is the lightest of blues. I've never seen this in werewolves, humans yes, but not werewolves. It's strange...but oddly fascinating and extremely beautiful.

And second, the faint but clearly obvious old scars that run over her right eye. The light pink noticeable against her pale complexion, the three jagged lines go from her hairline down across the eye, and curve towards her ear before stopping at the bottom of her ear.

They are definitely from a werewolf raking his claws over her face, from how deep they are and the fact that didn't disappear completely, it must have been extremely painful.

They do not mar her beauty though, but oddly make her more...mysterious and unique. But it still doesn't take away from the anger I feel for the wolf who did this to her.

"How did you get these?" I ask as I gently trace over the old injury with my thumb.

"I-I don't remember..." she murmurs, a look of slight frustration and despair on her face.

"You don't?"

She shakes her head in response.

"I don't really remember much from my time as a pup...other than my mom...I just remember that I had these before my first shift."

I tuck the rest of her hair behind her ears, absorbing the information and choosing to not ask anymore questions for now. The sadness in her eyes hurting my heart, I grab the bowl from the counter with one hand and lift her chin with the other.

"How about we eat before it gets cold?"

She smiles at me, and I return the gesture. My mind already fully consumed with her mystery.

~~THREE~~

To , who has a love for the Second Chance stories. I hope you like this one just as much!

Fleura

The smell of eggs and sausage pull me from my sleep, along with the scent of pancakes and coffee...

Still half asleep, I roll out of bed and start padding towards the source. My oversized red t-shirt almost covering my black sleep shorts completely. The wood floor is cold to my bare feet, and I yawn as I push my messy hair from in front of my face, the bedhead is real this morning. I'm definitely going to need at least ten minutes to comb it out. Walking into the kitchen, I halt to a stop at the sight in front of me.

A handsome, shirtless Dakota cooking breakfast. His long hair is pulled into a hair tie that I let him borrow, the soft locks pulled over his shoulder. His back faces me, giving me a good look at the black wing tattoos starting from his broad shoulders, and down his muscular back to his hips with the sweatpants hanging low on them.

Oh Goddess, I think I'm drooling.

"Are you just going to stare, Flower? Or are you going to eat?"

His deep voice snaps me from my ogling, and I look up to meet his dark brown eyes, which are equally ogling me back...making me a little bit self-conscious. I nervously go to try to smooth out my wild hair, and the sound of his throaty chuckle brings a flush of embarrassment to my cheeks.

"Don't be embarrassed Flower, it's a good look on you..."

Something in his voice makes me shiver, and I search for anything that could distract me from his presence, which in itself is difficult. He's much taller than I originally thought now that he's been standing next to me. I flick my eyes towards his large hands...another mistake since he's turned around, his bare chest facing me instead of his back.

"Is something the matter little one? You're awfully red."

His tone is both concerned and teasing, and I wouldn't be surprised if he was smirking right now.

And who's fault is that?

I think to myself as Aurora stirs awake, and the sight of Dakota in front of us sends her purring, much to my embarrassment. I just know he heard it, Goddess he's going to think I'm a horny she wolf if I keep behaving like this.

~Well...we kind of are. Just look at him.~

The sound of Aurora's quiet voice surprises me. She honestly doesn't talk too much, I can feel her emotions and understand them, but she usually doesn't talk unless she needs to. But since we've been in Dakota's presence, she talked a whole lot more.

"Flower?"

I jump at the feeling of a hand on my cheek, the warm tingles that erupt anytime me and this man touch blooming wildly under my skin. He tilts my chin upwards, bringing my gaze back to his. His intense stare turns me impossibly redder, and the softest of growls comes from his smirking mouth.

"Your wolf is showing Flower."

Surprised, I frantically feel along my head to figure out what he means, thinking it was my ears...and then when I found my normal human ones, I thought maybe he meant a tail. Before I could check for that though, he laughs and grabs my hands. An amused smile brightening his face as laughter rumbles deeply from his chest.

"No Flower, your eyes. Your eyes have turned gold."

"Oh...I see.." I squeak out, mortified that I just made an utter fool of myself. Aurora must have gotten temporarily excited about him.

"You are so adorable, it's unbearable."

I bite my lip, and another soft growl rumbles from Dakota. I swear his brown eyes turn pitch black for a split second, but he closes them and steps back...reluctantly?

"Go ahead and fix you a plate, I'm going to go take a shower first. Are there some spare clothes I can borrow?"

"They're in the guest bedroom...I didn't know long you'd need to stay and heal."

He opens his eyes again, a soft look in them now.

"Thank you Fleura. I don't know if I would've survived if you hadn't helped me."

"It's okay...you saved me first." I whisper, not really used to praise.

He raises a hand to my cheek, brushing his knuckles across it softly. After which he walks towards the bathroom, leaving me alone in the kitchen with the food he prepared. I begin fixing my plate, filling it with pancakes, sausage and scrambled eggs. I make my coffee with milk and sugar, pinching a bit of cinnamon into the mix as well as I almost drown my pancakes in maple syrup.

I eat and drink quietly as I listen to the water run in the shower, but I notice the time is ten minutes to nine, and I scarf down the rest of my food before I take off towards my room in haste. My shift at the library starts at 9:30, I can't be late.

I hurriedly brush through my hair, sleeping with it damp making it curly. I try throw it in a ponytail before giving up and going for a messy bun, letting my bangs fall over my scar. I pull on a pair of jeans and a brown long sleeve shirt, then one of my favorite pairs of ankle boots.

I grab my purse and fly out my bedroom, only to collide into Dakota...who's wearing nothing but a towel around his hips. His long hair wet and dripping down his chest and back. I wrench my eyes away from his body and stumble back.

"I-I'm so s-sorry!" I stutter out.

How many times can I embarrass myself in one hour?

"It's alright little one, are you leaving?"

I nod. "I have to go to work at the library. My shift starts in twenty minutes."

"Oh, would it be alright if I come with you? My truck is actually in town with my things in it."

"Sure, just...hurry please. I don't want to be late."

I ask as I keep my eyes down, edging my way towards the kitchen slowly.

"Of course, I'll be right out."

The sound of the guest room door closing lets me know that I can look up again, I go to put away all the food for later, leaving out some for Dakota to eat along the way. After that I go to stand by the back door, waiting for him to finish getting dressed.

His truck and belongings...does that mean he's leaving? I mean, it's only logical now that he's healed...and he no doubt has to go back home to his pack...but...

I don't want him to go...and that surprises me. I've known him all of twenty four hours, never lived anyway but by myself, and I'm so painfully shy that it's almost impossible for me to get close to anyone but...I want him to stay with me...

Just the idea of being away from him is unbearable, like there is a magnetic pull between us that'll cause me pain if it's fought.

Why do I feel this way? Does he feel it too? Or is it just me?

"Fleura?"

I jump at the sound of Dakota's voice, and I turn to see him wearing a pair of jeans that are a bit snug and a black shirt that stretches taunt over his chest. The necklace with the wolf pendant lays over his shirt, and his long hair is pulled back into a low ponytail, still a bit damp.

"Are you alright Flower?"

I blush at the nickname, liking it when he calls me that.

"I'm fine..." I look down at the floor, noticing his feet are bare. "Oh, you don't have any shoes."

"I have some in my truck, the ones I had been wearing ripped to shreds the last time I shifted." He assures, a smile in his voice.

"Sorry about the clothes, I didn't know what size so I just guessed."

"Don't worry, its fine. Lets go now, you don't want to be late now, do you?"

With that we exit the back door, and get into my battered old truck. The ancient relic rumbles loudly as we ride the dirt path up to the road and then into town, and I pull into the parking lot of the library after he assures that his truck is actually next door in the motel parking lot.

We both get out and head to our destinations, me to the library and him to his truck, and I enter the library with a heavy heart, and Aurora whimpering at my worried thoughts.

Dakota

I watch Fleura enter the old library from inside my truck, her head hung low with sadness in her expression. Why does she look so sad?

~Because she thinks we're leaving her...~ Zayev replies, his voice a bit hurt as well.

~Why would she think that?~

~Think about it dumbass. We're healed, we have our truck and all our belongings, and we told her we are the Gamma of our pack. She thinks we're going home because it's logical.~

Of course...she put that together after I asked her to bring me here for my truck. With her not knowing that I'm her mate, all she knows is that

I'm more than likely leaving and she's hurting because of it. She probably doesn't even understand why she's hurting...oh my sweet little Flower.

~We have to tell her Zayev.~

~Agreed.~

I crank up my truck and pull into the library parking lot, pulling in beside her rusty truck and parking. I jump into my backseat, thanking the goddess for tinted windows and a large truck as I change out of the ill fitting clothes and into some of my own. A brown long sleeve shirt, a pair of dark blue jeans, and my socks and boots.

As I pull the sleeves up on my arm, my cellphone rings inside my duffle bag. I fish it out and check the number, and for the first time in over a year I'm happy to see it.

Alpha Jacob.

I press answer and press it to my ear, prepared to surprise the poor bastard by actually answering the phone.

"Hello Jake."

"My Goddess, its about damn time you answered my calls. Where the hell are you?"

I chuckle, the reaction exactly what I expected it to be.

"In Minnesota, its long story."

"It better be a good one too, do you know how worried sick everyone has been? Your sisters? Your mother? Beta Paul and Amy? Me? Especially Jessica? Goddess Dakota, it's been a year since you've talked to any of us. We were worried you were dead!"

I sigh in resignation, knowing he's right. His mate and Amy look at me like a little brother, and my three baby sisters should be almost shifting age by now...goddess, my mom. She's probably scared to death...if not furious. Time to be honest.

"Well, the truth is...I found my mate...."

"Come on Kota, I'm happy for you but you know damn well that isn't-"

"A year ago Jake, she rejected me because I wasn't an Alpha..."

It goes quiet after my interruption, and I'm pretty sure I can hear the muted sounds of gasps and voices...no doubt the whole office is full of the people he mentioned.

"I'm sorry Kota, I didn't know...so that's why you've been gone so long."

I sigh, a smile forming on my lips as I plan my answer.

"Yeah...but that's over now. I'm coming home."

"You are? Don't get me wrong, I'm glad you are but...why? What changed?"

I grin wider, knowing my mom is probably going to scream with joy at this.

"I found my Second Chance Jake...I found my second mate..."

A high pitched squeal echoes on the opposite end of the phone, and I pull it away from my ear like it's a dangerous weapon. I can tell mom isn't the only one who's excited, but Jake interrupts.

"I'm happy for you man. Who is she?"

"Her name is Fleura, and she's a gypsy wolf, but I have a feeling she'd make an excellent pack doctor. I plan on bringing her with me when I come home, so please be prepared. And warn my mother when she calms down that Fleura is really shy and not accustomed to pack life."

"I will, and make sure you come home soon, we're all looking forward to catching up."

"I will, and tell my family I'll be expecting some brownies after I take their beating."

He laughs. "Sure thing man, see you soon."

"See you guys." I say before I hang up.

Putting the phone in my pocket, I put my wallet in my back pocket and clip my keys to my belt loop. I get out my truck and lock it, planning to explore the library and find my sweet little mate.

I have a lot to explain.

~~FOUR~~

I seem to have a very elusive mate.

I had decided to wait until Fleura's lunch break to talk to her, which according to the older woman who is her boss, started ten minutes ago. After her boss, who was not so subtle about the fact she found me attractive, told me typical places where my mate spent her lunch break, I went in search.

First was the burger joint across the street, then the coffee shop, and finally was the park.

Being that I had already went to the other two, I'm pretty sure she's at the park. I spot her fairly quickly as I pull in, sitting at a covered area eating her lunch while reading. I smile and get out, keeping my eyes on her as I follow her delicious scent.

"Mind if I join you Flower?"

I murmur in her ear after reaching her, making her jump in surprise as that familiar blush stains her face a beautiful shade of red.

"Da-Dakota! You're still here?"

Her honest surprise and enthusiasm fills me with happiness, the fact that she's happy to see me and wants me to stay makes me and Zayev want to howl.

"Of course I am. Why would I leave?"

She bites her lip again, shyly averting her gaze. As much as I love her bashful reactions, I wish she didn't hide her eyes from me. I love how wide and expressive they are, practically saying exactly how she's feeling.

"I thought you had to go home...you have a pack that needs you..."

I brush her bangs out of her eyes, exposing both of their depths to me.

"Actually, there is something much more important at the moment. Would you like to go on a walk with me?"

Tilting her head in that adorable way, she looks a bit confused, and I honestly can't blame her.

"I want to talk to you about something important...please Flower?" I plead softly.

She nods, and I smile triumphantly as she throws her trash away and pulls her purse over her shoulder. As we begin walking, I notice how she keeps inching closer to me almost instinctively, only to shy away once she notices our proximity. Determined to keep her close, when she edges closer I softly grab her hand, and she jumps in surprise as I intertwine our fingers.

"Dakota?" She squeaks, a I smile down at her softly.

"You keep wandering away from me Flower, I just want to keep you close."

Her face blooms a healthy shade of crimson, and I can hear her heartbeat accelerate even faster. The sparks she's feeling are most definitely impacting her, and I have a feeling that her wolf is stirred up as well...Zayev certainly is.

"Where...where are we going?" She asks curiously, and she walks even closer to me

"Somewhere quiet, I want to talk to you where we won't be overheard by human ears."

I murmur the last part, and she nods, knowing that it was best to keep out of human earshot when talking about werewolves. After arriving to the edge of the park, where a large garden of wildflowers grow in bright and varied colors, we stop. And despite the beauty of the nature that surrounds us, I find that the most beautiful flower is the one standing beside me.

~As much as I agree with you boy, you are getting sappier by the minute.~ Zayev rumbles, and I smirk. He is right, but I don't see it as something to be ashamed of. Mates are supposed to bring out the best in each other, so if my best is a little sappy, so be it.

"So...what did you want to talk about Dakota?"

Fleura's soft voice pulls me from my thoughts, and I discretely sniff the air, pleased that there isn't a human scent anywhere...and that the only werewolf I smell is her.

"I wanted to ask you something about mates, Flower."

I start, ignoring my wolfs demands to just blurt out the truth. I need to explain and break this gently, she'll have too many doubts otherwise.

"Mates?"

"Mhm, mates. You see, I've been wondering something since the day I woke up on your couch."

She waits for me to continue, and I do.

"It's about when I asked you if you had a mate. Even though you said no, you hesitated for a moment, like you were uncertain. I was wondering why that is."

Keeping her hand in mine, I turn so that I'm standing in front of her, her short stature even tinier next to mine. A stressed look in her eyes worries me, and I brush my thumb over her cheek.

"Because...because my wolf was saying ye-yes, and I didn't know why."

I smile broadly, my excitement starting to show through my face.

"I can explain to you why."

Her eyes widen in surprise, her hand squeezing mine tighter in response.

"You can?"

"Yes...it's not that difficult."

"Okay...what's the reason then?"

I exhale in an attempt to calm myself, take it slow, don't rush it...make it enjoyable for her.

"When a wolf finds their mate, a few things begin to happen."

I begin, leaning down to talk directly in her ear, and she shivers as my breath fans over her flushed skin. I inhale deeply, not hiding the moan that her mouthwatering aroma brings out of me.

"First, the individual who is your mate gives off a intoxicating scent that draws you in, its aroma becoming almost the only scent you notice...one that you can smell anywhere no matter how faint it is...and when it's close, you feel like you're blissfully drowning in it."

Her breath hitches a bit, and I continue, looking into her two colored eyes deeply.

"Second, when you lay your eyes on them for the first time, your wolf drives you to get closer, to investigate the softness of their hair... the beauty of their eyes...the freckles that are dusted over their cheeks..."

Finally, I trail my fingers slowly down her face, from her temple to her cheek...and softly down her neck...her body shivers under my touch, and I can't help but feel both proud and honored to be the one who makes her react this way.

"When that happens, and the two mates finally touch...warm sparks erupt where their skin touches, a pleasant sensation that makes them want to keep going...to keep making their mate feel good by their hands...an almost magnetic pull that's nearly impossible to resist."

My hand stops at the crook of her shoulder, tracing small, continuous circles around the place I'd mark her, the place that will always be one of the most sensitive for her from now on. Soft gasps escape from her parted lips, and I remind myself that I have to restrain myself at the moment...her enjoying this doesn't mean that she understands what I'm telling her.

I loosen my other hand from her tight grasp, and brush over her lips with the tips of my fingers...revealing in how soft and warm they are.

"Da-Dakota..."

I growl lowly at how she says my name, her voice shaky and panting...almost pleading. Her tiny hands grip my shirt tightly, shaking as my teasing persists.

"I know this because this is exactly what I felt when I first inhaled your scent Flower, when I looked into your eyes...the first time you touched me...for the past couple of days it's all I could think about."

I remove my hands from her skin to place them on her covered shoulders, and her whimper at the loss of my touch nearly makes me return to teasing her. Almost...I need to make sure she understands, that she knows what this means.

"I know this because you are my mate Fleura... and I am yours."

Her eyes widen in shock, her heartbeat racing at a breakneck pace.

"I-I am? But I thought...but you said...don't you already..?"

Her convoluted, unfinished sentences may sound like gibberish, but I can understand her confusion. I told her that I found my mate a year ago...so she's confused as to how I can be hers.

"In the werewolf world, sometimes our first mate isn't the right fit...sometimes they reject us...that's why the Goddess gave us the ability to find another mate... a second chance at love. They are called Second Chance mates...and Flower, you are mine."

An unexpected sadness pools in her eyes, and I begin to panic.

"So I'm just an apology? I'm only your mate because the one you were meant to love chose to reject you?"

I cup her cheeks, trying to keep her from crying.

"No Flower! No, you aren't an apology, or a consolation prize, you are my soulmate. You always were. I never felt this way with that she wolf because she never gave me a chance."

Her soft sniffles break my heart, the fact that I made her cry is unbearable.

"She rejected me before she even knew my name, the only thing I felt for her was heartache. Sweetheart, I never would've been happy with her...because she never would've been happy with me."

Her watery eyes gaze up at me, a slight hopeful look in them giving me hope as well.

"You aren't second place Fleura, you were always first. It just required me having my heart broken to find you...and it was worth it."

Her fingers reach up to touch my cheek, and I sigh at the contact. This is the first time she's touched me outside of accident or necessity, and it feels wonderful.

"I wish you didn't have to suffer to find me...it doesn't seem fair." She murmurs, her expression almost guilty.

"It lead me to you Flower, and for that I am grateful. So do not feel guilty about it, it's the way the Goddess meant for it to be."

I pull her against me, wrapping my arms around her as I inhale her scent. After a moment her arms embrace me as well, at least, they attempt to. Her arms not quite long enough to reach around me completely. I run my hands up and down her back as we hold each other, and her wolfy purr rumbles through my chest.

"Is that why you didn't go home? Because I'm your...mate?" She asks after a few minutes of silence.

"That, and because I didn't want to leave until you were ready to come with me."

She pulls back to look up at me, her eyes full of questions.

"Come with you?"

I chuckle, brushing her hair behind her ears.

"To my home. To live with me in my pack as my mate, and meet my family. I know you don't have much experience with pack life...so I wanted to wait until you were ready before I go home."

She seems to think about my words thoroughly, a bit conflicted before smiling up at me, the sight beautiful to my eyes.

"Why not now?"

I blink a couple of times before I can process her question.

"You really want to go this soon? We don't have to rush."

"I know...but I want to. I would love to see your home and meet your family. I know it might be a bit overwhelming...but I can handle it as long I can stay with you..."

Her cheeks are dusted pink as she finishes, and I can feel Zayev's urge to shift and run around like an excited puppy. Instead, I press soft kisses all over her face before grazing over her lips. As much as I would love to kiss her senseless, we need to take baby steps, and give her time to adjust and grow comfortable with me.

"You have no idea how happy that makes me. And don't you worry, I'll be by your side through the entire thing."

~~FIVE~~

It's time for a new chapter!!! Above is what Dakota and Fleura's home looks like. Enjoy!!"~~~~~~

Fleura

To say I am extremely nervous is an understatement.

Sitting in the passenger seat of Dakota's truck, I anxiously play with my hair. It was a week before we left Minnesota because I had to sell my ancient truck, and once I finally did that, Dakota helped me pack up my personal possessions from the house I was renting. Now after a day of traveling, we're only an hour away from Dakota's pack in Missouri, the Starry Creek pack consisting of the entire state as their territory...

200 wolves...so many new faces...

As the truck stops at a red light, Dakota's hand rests gently on my skirt covered knee, and I look up to see him gazing at me.

"You don't need to be nervous Flower, they will love you."

I avert my gaze shyly, a blush undoubtedly on my face. I wish I wasn't so bashful around him, it would probably make things easier for the both of us if I wasn't. So, after a bit of deliberation, I reach for his hand and lay mine on top of it...the pleasant feeling of warm tingling in my palm making my cheeks hotter. I hear his slight rumble of approval, so he must have liked it as well...I do remember him enjoying when I touched his cheek in the park that day...and when I played with his hair yesterday and this morning, braiding the long locks in a thick braid. Which much to my surprise, he actually liked, and kept after insisting that he loved it.

Peeking at him from the corner of my eye, I watch the wind that's coming through the rolled down windows blow through the loose strands that were too short to stay in place. His soft smile accentuates the dimple on his chin, and the light reflecting in eyes turn them from dark brown to a whiskey color...so pretty...

"I can feel your beautiful eyes on me Flower, if you want to sit closer you can, you don't have to ask."

He murmurs as he turns the truck onto the next road, and I drop my gaze again.

Come on Fleura, you can do this.

Taking a reassuring breath, I quickly unbuckle my seatbelt on the passenger seat and slide over to the middle seat, buckling that seatbelt on before I can change my mind. I lean into Dakota's side, and he moves his hand from my knee to drape his right arm over my shoulders...that purring sound rumbling louder as his fingers absentmindedly twirl my hair.

"I think you're going to love the pack land Flower, rivers run through the territory, and there are meadows full of wildflowers and a clearing that has a pond full of water lilies and fish. My home...actually our home now..."

His eyes flicker to me for a moment before going back to the road, but his broad smile remains. I can see the happiness in his eyes, and I can feel the simultaneous swell of happiness in my chest at the idea of sharing a home with him.

"Well, our home has a river practically in the backyard, and even though it is close to the pack house, it's set off so it's more private. My mom, and sisters live nearby too, so we can have visits with each other."

It sounds wonderful, and since he told me about his family I've wondered what they were like. He's shown me pictures and told me stories, but I still wonder what they are like in person.

The girls are actually 12 year old triplets, which is apparently rare in werewolves. Twins aren't uncommon, but triplets are.

Rain is the oldest by two minutes, she's fond of painting and drawing, and is very adventurous. Always has paint on her hands or on her face, and she likes to paint abstract over realistic.

Calla is second, she loves playing sports and has a knack for getting dirty in the cleanest of places. And when she isn't running through the mud and playing with the football, she's doing little fashion shows...happy to say that there is no reason a girl can't do both.

And finally there is Fawn, she has a great love of reading and writing, and is really good at science and math. She's also like me, a bit shy around new people, so she and I will either hit it off first or be the last to connect.

All three have Dakota's complexion, and their hair is black instead of dark brown, but they each have different eye colors. Rain has blue, Calla has hazel, and Fawn has gray.

"It sounds beautiful. Have your sisters shifted yet?" I ask curiously, and he shakes his head.

"Not yet, though they should once they reach thirteen. All three of them are excited by that, and so is mom...but I'm equally anxious as well as excited...I guess the idea of them growing up kinda scares me a little."

I smile, finding his protective big brother instincts cute...and admirable.

"You're their big brother...you're always going to worry about them..."

He chuckles.

"You're right...Goddess help me when they get old enough to find their mates."

I laugh with him, and as we pass through the towns and small cities, he shows me a few of the sights...explaining the history behind each one. I have to say, as fascinating as the landmarks were, I was mostly focused on the way his deep voice said everything. More interested in the way he told the stories and how much he enjoyed telling them...

When we finally pass through Jefferson City and make it to Vienna, I'm drawn to how many trees surround us as we drive. I know where I lived in Minnesota was wooded, but compared to this it's practically sparse in comparison.

And it's not just the trees...it's the water too. We've crossed over and passed by so much water, some rivers we saw multiple times due to how they were curved and moved. A few minutes after driving out of the city, we turn off the paved road and onto a dirt trail that disappears into the thick section of trees on the side of the road.

"We're still a couple minutes away from the pack house, but I officially welcome you to Starry Creek, Flower."

As I gaze out the windshield, I notice a gray wolf standing near the path, watching us for a moment before disappearing into the trees.

"Looks like we've been spotted, so much for a surprise."

Dakota chuckles out, and start feeling a little nervous again. I don't know if I'm ready to enter the pack house yet.

"Don't worry sweetheart, we're not going to the pack house first. I'm going to take us to our home, that way we can get settled and you can meet everyone slowly before going to the pack house. I've asked my family and the Alpha and Beta to give us a bit of time before coming over."

I internally sigh in relief, thankful that he somehow could read my mind. We continue driving through the territory, following the bumpy dirt path as Dakota takes me to our new home, pointing out the other buildings and the pack house as we passed them. When we finally arrive at what I assume is our new home, I can only stare in shock.

It's incredible...

With at least two stories, it's exterior is designed with both red brick and blue siding, and a large stone fireplace sits in front instead of on the side. It has a covered porch where two rocking chairs and an outdoor table sit, a pot of vibrant flowers sits on the table and rose bushes grow in the grass in front of the porch. As I stare in awe, Dakota chuckles, turning into the driveway and parking beside the large house.

"You like it Flower?"

I turn to him, still surprised.

"Is this really your home?"

He cups my cheek in his hand.

"Our home Fleura, it's our home now."

My heart picks up speed at his words, and I look at the house again in muted excitement.

Our home...I like the sound of that.

We exit the truck after a moment, and Dakota insists on taking my bags even as he flips through his keys. Unlocking the front door, he turns to me with a bit of a sheepish expression on his face.

"It's been a little while since I've lived here...so it might be a bit messy...and dusty..."

I giggle, trying not to imagine how messy it could be as he opens the door.

Looking inside, I'm met with the sight of a very open space, its wine red and golden beige walls giving it a warm and welcoming feeling. The cream colored carpet and dark wood furniture compliments well with the design, and the living room section on my left has a brown leather sofa and a pair of tan love seats sit facing each other of it in front of the fireplace. A crotchet blanket lays over the back of the couch with a couple of beige pillows, and a ceiling fan hangs idly from the ceiling.

To my left is the dining room, with a dark wood table big enough for eight people, with a small crystal chandelier hanging over it. The red table runner sitting in the middle has a bronze deer statue in between a pair of candlesticks, and the table is set with eight place settings.

I have to be honest...it's not quite the 'bachelor pad' I was expecting, and it's not at all messy, there isn't even any dust on the furniture. But I guess I haven't seen the whole house yet, there may be a man cave somewhere in here.

"It's beautiful Dakota..." I say honestly, and he chuckles.

"Thank you, but it's probably my mothers doing. I recall there being some stray clothes on the couch, and a few open books on the table instead of dinnerware when I was here last. She probably came in and cleaned up while I was gone instead of just feeding my pet turtle like I asked."

My ears perk at the word turtle, and I turn to face him excitedly.

"You have a turtle?"

"Yeah, a red eared slider named Shilo. Do you like turtles?"

I nod vigorously, and he grins.

"Then I'll show him to you after we settle in. But first, why don't I show you the rest of the house?"

I follow him around the place curiously, him holding my hand tightly as I explore after putting our things inside the house. The kitchen is sleek and modern, with white marble counter tops, dark wood cabinets and stainless steel appliances. It turns out his mother also had been keeping the food in check and tossing out the old stuff, which Dakota was happy about, saying something about never wanting to think about how rancid year old expired milk would smell.

Upstairs was amazing too, mostly because I never lived in a house that was more than one story before. The wooden stairs lead up to the second floor, which is almost completely the opposite of the theme downstairs.

Light blue walls in the hallways, plush gray carpet, and silver wolves stenciled onto the light blue paint. There are four moderate sized bedrooms, and a good sized bathroom is near the top of the stairs.

When I asked why the four guest rooms had blank walls and no furniture other than a bed, he just looked at me longingly and explained that they would be redecorated for future children.

To say I turned fire engine red was an understatement...the idea of having children with him making me both extremely nervous and excited...I tried to ignore that though, but failed miserably when he showed me the largest room on the second floor at the end of the hall...the master bedroom...

Our bedroom...

Just the thought brought back the flustered thoughts I just pushed back, flooding my mind with inappropriate images that surprise me. Since when have I been so...so...

"Flower?"

Dakota calls, snapping me from my bizarre daydreaming. I need to put a stop to those things...it's not good for my heart.

"Are you alright?"

He asks, brushing a piece of hair from my eyes.

"I'm fine...just a little distracted..."

He nods, and I return to surveying the room. The silver gray walls are accented with beige, and a king size bed with gray and white bedding sits opposite of the door, the large window behind it casting a soft light into the room. A black circular nightstand sits on either side of the bed, each with a lamp and alarm clock on them. The floor is vinyl instead of wood or carpet, and its design makes it appear as dark blue stone tile, and a cream colored plush rug sits under the bed.

There's a bookshelf full of books on one side between a pair of doors, and a computer desk sits between a pair of dressers on the opposite side. A large TV sits on a black stand on one side of the door, and a small, dark blue couch sits on the other with white pillows on it.

"Do you like it?" He murmurs, a bit worried.

I nod, liking the look of the room...even if I've never been in a bedroom this big.

"I'm glad. The door on the right of the bookcase is our closet, I already have space set for you in it as well as the dresser on the right of the desk. The door on the left is for our bathroom, you can look around while I bring our things up....oh, and the room upstairs is small, but it's more of a game or movie room if you want to go up there too."

I remember the stairs near the bathroom that go up and nod, and he smiles and kisses me on the forehead before going downstairs. I go to the closet and peek inside first after taking off my ballet flats, noting the empty side Dakota said was for me as I smile and go to the bathroom to look around.

It's pretty big, with white stone tile that's cold to my bare feet, and sea green walls, there's both a garden tub and a walk in shower, with a pair of raised sinks with marble countertops next to the toilet. A stack of towels sit on a table between the doorway and shower, with a set of dark green ones hanging from the towel rack above it.

"Definitely moms doing, this place was a mess the last time I saw it."

I jump at the sound of my mates voice behind me, and I turn to watch him place a bag on the counter between the sinks.

"She probably didn't want you to see that, thinking it might scare you off."

I laugh, and he chuckles with me. But our moment is interrupted by the sound of the doorbell ringing.

"I'll get it Flower, you can go explore some more."

He goes back downstairs, and I quickly head upstairs to the tiny floor. The room is blank walled with multiple leather beanbag chairs circling around a TV which is connected to a game station and a DVD player. I also saw the turtle tank with Shilo in it, and I gaze at the little creature as he sits on his basking rock.

The sound of muted voices downstairs sends a bit of nervousness through me, and I count about five different heartbeats not including Dakotas.

"Flower? Can you come downstairs please?" Dakota calls up from the stairs.

I swallow hard and make my way downstairs, my heart racing as I do.

~~SIX~~

Dakota

I head downstairs to answer the door, leaving my mate to explore the house. I wasn't expecting visitors this soon, so I don't have a real idea of who it is.

I reach the front door and open it, and I'm immediately engulfed in a hug.

"Dakota!!! My baby!!!"

My mothers cry of joy is easy to recognize, and I can't help but be happy to see her again. I return her embrace carefully, not wanting to crush the small she wolf in my arms. Sometimes it's hard to believe that this tiny 5'3 woman gave birth to 6'5 me..

I look behind her to see four more familiar faces:

Alpha Jacob and his mate Luna Jessica, and Beta Paul and his mate Beta Amy. They haven't changed a bit since the last time I saw them, and the two women rush up to me, assisting my mother in trapping me.

"Hey mom...Luna, Beta Amy. You do realize I'm not going anywhere this time, right?"

"You better not! I promise that if you even try to leave like that ever again I'll find you and beat the shit out of you!!!" Jessica threatens, and I can't help but feel a little nervous at my human Luna's wrath. Jacob laughs behind her, and Paul joins him.

"I'm with Jessica, you'll have to deal with us if you do that again!!" Amy adds, her tiny arms squeezing even tighter around me. The little red headed she wolf has only gotten even feistier since I saw her last.

"And I'm going to drag you back home by the ears after they're finished." Mom finishes, looking up at me with seriousness in her blue eyes.

"I promise mom, I'm not going anywhere now."

"Good. Now let me meet the girl! I want to see your second chance mate!"

I chuckle at her enthusiasm, and after the girls let me go, they proceed to giving me the puppy dog look as well.

"Sorry man, we tried to keep them away, but you know they wouldn't have lasted long." Paul chuckles nervously, and I sigh. I wanted to give Fleura some time to adjust to being here...but maybe having some friends and faces she could recognize could help her adjust quicker...

"Alright...wait in the living room...I'll get Fleura."

The girls cheer excitedly before rushing inside, Paul and Jacob shaking their heads as they follow their hyper mates. I follow after them and start towards the stairs to the second floor sitting above the washer and dryer in the wash room. I stop and turn towards the living room, locking eyes with my mother.

"Please. Fleura is shy, and nervous around new wolves, so try not to overwhelm her, okay?"

I turn back and start up the stairs, listening intently to the sound of my mates nervous heartbeat, no doubt she already heard the visitors come inside.

"Flower, can you come downstairs please?"

Her soft padding footsteps start heading down the stairs, and she meets me halfway down. Her pink floral skirt swishes around her calves, the chiffon soft against her skin. Her brown fitted tank top matches it perfectly, and the beaded belt hangs slanted over her hips.

"Dakota? Who's here?" She whispers softly, her fingers combing through her blonde hair nervously. I grab her hand and tuck the pale locks behind her ear with the rest that's held back by her braided leather headband.

"My Mom is here. As well as Alpha Jacob and his mate Luna Jessica, and the Betas Paul and Amy. They all wanted to see me...and meet you."

She nibbles on her bottom lip, which has become very distracting habit to me.

"Now, if you're not ready to meet all of them yet, I understand. We can meet them another time if you like...there's no rush."

I cradle her cheek in my palm, and she sighs.

"It's okay...I want to meet them..." She murmurs.

"You sure?" I ask, and she nods.

I smile, taking her hand in mine and slowly lead her down the stairs, she stays close behind me, hiding a bit from the guests she'll soon meet. As we reach the bottom, she stops and attempts to cover the faint scar over her right eye, and I automatically stop her.

"You don't have to hide behind your hair flower, you are beautiful."

Her blush makes me grin, and we continue through the kitchen and head towards the living room, my little mate staying mostly behind me. The voices turn to shushed whispers as we close in at the entrance, at I can see my mother is about to explode out of her chair as I edge around the corner.

"Guys, this is Fleura."

I gently coax her out from behind my back, and she squeezes my hand tightly as she peeks at the small crowd in front of us. My moms face turns into that familiar sappy, melting one that she has whenever she sees a newborn pup, or an actual puppy. And I can't blame her, Fleura is adorable...

Fleura glances at my mom for a moment before turning to the others nervously, no doubt feeling the immense power radiating of all of them combined. For a wolf who's only met a Gamma, being in the same room as an Alpha, Luna, and the Beta pair, along with her Gamma mate must be a bit overwhelming. So when she leans into my chest, I curl an arm around her protectively. I know that no one in this room would even think about hurting her, but if it helps her feel safe I'll do it.

"Hello dear, my name is Nayely Jackson. It's so lovely to meet you."

My mom smiles softly as she walks up to us, noticeably holding back her excitement over meeting Fleura.

"Hello Miss Jackson..."

My mom chuckles. "You don't have to be so formal darling, just call me Nay, or Ellie."

~She is so precious baby...I can hardly stand it!!~ Mom internally squeals through the mind link.

~I know mom...she's perfect...~

Fleura nods, and looks up to see Jessica and Amy behind my mom.

"I'm Luna Jessica and this is Amy, but you can just call me Jess. It's really nice to meet you."

My mate shakes the brunettes hand as well as Amy's, and a bit of pride swells in my chest.

"And I'm Alpha Jacob, and this is Beta Paul. It's a pleasure to meet you Miss Fleura."

She gives my Alpha and Beta a small smile, and they decide not to hold out their hands like the rest, probably noticing that she's more timid around them than anyone else in the room.

~Who knew that the gruff, no nonsense Gamma that pushed warriors to their limits would end up with such a shy mate?~ Paul snickers internally, and Jacob laughs.

~I guess the saying really is true, opposites do attract..~

I let an irritated growl through the mind link, making sure that a single bit of it doesn't leak out into the room. I don't recall having ever growled in front of Fleura, but I'm not going to start now when she is already so anxious.

They both go quiet at that, and just as I think it was about to become an awkward silence, mom gasps in shock, her hands flying over her mouth for a moment.

"I was so excited to see you darling that I forgot about the lasagnas I made!! They should be almost be done by now!! I'll be right back!!"

She sprints out of the room faster than I think would be possible, and I can see Fleura's bewildered expression physically echoing my thoughts.

"I guess it might be a bit soon to ask if we could come over for lunch?" Jessica inquires, but before I can respond I notice Fleura nodding her head.

"That would be nice...right Dakota?"

I smile down at her affectionately, her tiny blush warming her face beautifully.

"That sounds perfect Flower." I reply, brushing over her cheek softly with my thumb. I cast a look at the girls when I hear their simultaneous 'awws', and the guys have a look in their eyes that promises attempted blackmail and teasing later.

"Great. And of course your mom cooked your favorite homemade lasagna, so you know it's going to be good." Amy adds, clasping her hands together in excitement. And speaking of the devil, mom comes in through the door.

"Lunch is served everyone!!!"

~~~~~~~~~~~~

We ended up demolishing two of the three lasagnas my mom made, along with the salad and breadsticks Jessica and Amy prepared. I admit that I contributed the most to the consumption of the main course, considering it's been my favorite since I was little.

Though I will say that Fleura helped with that as well, even if she had only four pieces to my six...although she did eat more salad and breadsticks than I did.

It surprised the rest of the dinner party to see her keep up with me...which automatically made her flush with embarrassment, and even more so when I bragged about her cooking skills to my mom, telling her about the excellent beef stew and meatloaf she could whip up. My mom was unable to restrain herself from asking how Fleura was able to get me to eat meatloaf when she couldn't, explaining how I always turned my nose up at it as a kid.

Not too long after lunch, my sisters came here after being let out from school, and I was shocked at how much they've grown up in a year. They all were excited to see me, even Fawn was much more vocal than I was expecting...and they were all curious about Fleura, hitting it off with her very well.

Our dessert consisted of the brownies my sisters baked and brought over, and like expected, they didn't let me eat one until they had 'wolf piled' me and 'beat me' in a fight.

After our visitors finally left for the day, my mother nearly crushing me with a last hug and internally begging me to tell her the story of how Fleura and I met until I promised her I would, I was alone with my mate again at last. We ended up having dinner at a Mexican restaurant I love, deciding to save the leftover lasagna for later, and was happy to find that Fleura liked it too.

Now, we're home again, and with me returning to my duties as Gamma tomorrow, I need to turn in early...and I know that Fleura is tired after everything today. But, there seems to be something wrong.

"Fleura? Are you okay in there Flower?" I call out, knocking on the bathroom door. She's been quiet in there for a while after the shower turned off, but the sound of her feet patting softly onto the cool tile tells me she's pacing.

Her footsteps halt, and I half consider breaking the door lock to make sure she is okay.

"I'm fine...I'll be out in a moment..." She calls out, and I sigh and sit on the bed, staring at the flannel print on my pajama pants as I mull over her anxiety...what exactly could be bothering her?

My eyes flick towards the bathroom door as it opens, and it takes quite a bit of self restraint to keep myself seated. Zayev and I both growl at the sight of her wearing one of my T shirts, the black fabric hanging to her knees like a nightgown...Goddess she looks gorgeous...

"I hope it's okay...I left my pajamas in here, then I saw this sitting on the counter..." She trails off, turning red under my stare. I had decided to wear actual pajamas instead of just boxers, but later decided to skip the shirt and just pull on some bottoms...I forgot the shirt was even in there...

Clearing my throat, I try to control my less than helpful thoughts.

"You look...gorgeous..." I reply.

I honestly would have gone for tempting...or sexy...but I need to take this slow...she's nervous enough as it is.

Her eyes lower from mine in embarrassment, that distracting sight of her chewing on her bottom lip stirring me up even further.

The Goddess is truly testing me...

"Come on Flower, lets get some sleep."

I pat the space beside me on the bed, and she peeks up with that bashful expression I've come to adore.

"Come on sweetheart, I won't bite."

~Speak for yourself boy...I actually want to meet her wolf soon, and that will require us biting her.~ Zayev rumbles.

~I do too, but we're not doing it tonight, so muzzle it.~

~Careful who you bark at boy.~

Fleura slowly edges towards the bed, and as she climbs in and burrows under the covers, I chuckle.

"Come here you little chinchilla."

I pull her flush against my chest, her little squeak of surprise cute to my ears.

"Goodnight Fleura."

I murmur as I kiss the top of her head, to which she relaxes and cuddles closer to me, making me purr in satisfaction.

"Goodnight Dakota..."

Her voice muffled against my chest, I close my eyes and enjoy her warmth.

~~SEVEN~~

Fleura

Things have been going well the past month, and with the assistance of Luna Jessica and Beta Amy...as well as Dakota, I'm growing quite familiar with the life of a pack member, even if it was a bit overwhelming at first.

Thankfully, Dakota's pack doesn't officially have to do a ceremony to welcome me to the pack, just the Alpha's invitation is all that's needed, which I accepted...and my first shock was the numerous voices entering my thoughts through what Dakota called the 'pack mind link', which I've come to understand and tune out with my mates help.

Still, the first week was particularly challenging for me, because almost anytime I left the house I ended up lost...much to Dakota's amusement and concern. However, with the girls showing me the tricks to navigating the expansive area, and Dakota convincing me to go on wolf runs at night, I've figured out enough to manage...

In the process of these explorations, I've also seen where he trains the pack warriors...one of his main duties as gamma. I was a bit startled at first about how intense the fighting seemed, but he assured me it was only training to prepare for the real deal...that no one ever tried to intentionally injure each other, except when they were pissed with each other, but it didn't happen often.

Truthfully though, I found myself quite enamored with watching him train...me and my wolf both enjoying the view of our mate sweaty and wearing nothing but shorts. Dakota definitely seemed to pick up on that, so afterwards he would occasionally 'forget' his lunch at home so I would come down again, which was the reason I saw him the first time.

I do enjoy seeing him at lunch though, so if I see his food in the fridge I take it to him happily...along with mine so we can eat together.

Sighing, I hang the last shirt in the laundry basket on the clothesline, the warm breeze making it flap in the air along with the rest of me and Dakotas clothing. It's pretty hard to believe how much clothing he can go through in one day, and with both the dirt and grass stains, and the fact he didn't separate his clothes to wash them, I'm honestly surprised anything of his was clean...and void of color bleeding. From now on he's only allowed to fold laundry, which he is pretty good at and willing to do since I won't let him wash anything. I'm not taking a chance with my clothes, I spent my hard earned money on them after all.

Going inside the house through the back door, I take the basket upstairs to our bedroom to strip the bed, the sheets and blankets being next to wash. As I pull the pillowcases off of the pillows, yesterday's conversation with Jessica comes back to my thoughts.

"I'm honestly surprised that Dakota hasn't marked you yet, with him being so territorial and all."

I tilt my head in confusion, not quite sure what she's talking about.

"What do you mean?" I ask, and she chuckles.

"You haven't noticed? Most male wolves are so territorial over their mates, the higher ranked ones are the most. Don't you remember his reaction to those young warriors flirting with you last week? The growling and the death glare? I thought he was gonna go all Neanderthal 'my woman' on them." She laughs out the last part.

Now that she mentions it, he was quite possessive...and not just that day. He always seems to prefer to stay close to me, or hold my hand, or do that thing where he rubs under my chin like he would a cat...which makes me and Aurora purr much to my embarrassment, the main reason he does it so much....

And let's not forget how much he enjoys cuddling, which is adorable and enjoyable to me. I've spent almost every night falling asleep in his arms, and waking up in them with either my back or my head curled into his chest.

But it still doesn't explain the other thing she said.

"What does that have to do with the marking thing?"

Her eyes widen so much they nearly bug out of her head. What did I say?

"Oh my Goddess...you have no idea what marking is?" She replies with mute shock.

I shake my head, and she places her hands on my shoulders with an expression that makes me nervous.

"Marking is one of the most intimate acts between mates outside of actual mating. You're leaving a mark on your mate that will tell every wolf that they're yours and yours only."

Aurora softly purrs in my head, which makes me blush. The idea of mating with Dakota makes me a bit nervous...nervous, but not opposed in the slightest.

"How...does that work?"

She grins at my question.

"A special bite using your wolfs canines. It immediately leaves your scent mixing together with theirs, as well as establishing your own private mind link. And later, a unique mark appears on the skin where they were bitten." She explains, and her hand drifts to her own shoulder. My eyebrows furrow with deep thought at the image.

"A...bite? That sounds painful..."

She shakes her head. "Only for a split second, then its extremely pleasant for both parties..."

She holds a finger to her chin, tapping it as she thinks.

"It really is curious that he hasn't even brought it up with you though...I'd honestly think he'd want to do that pretty quickly."

I shake my head and go back to removing the sheets from our bed, taking the now full basket back to the washing machine under the stairs on the bottom floor.

He probably just hasn't thought about it...he has been busy with his duties as gamma...and he probably thought I'd already know what marking is...right?

After putting the sheets in and pouring in the detergent, I close the lid to the washing machine and cut it on, the sound of the water filling the machine pulling me back into that rainy day conversation.

"What are you thinking about so hard Flower?"

I jump and squeak at Dakota's voice, his strong arms circling around my waist from behind as he chuckles. I really must have been distracted if I didn't hear him come in.

"Just a conversation I had with Jess..."

I reply honestly, knowing that he could sniff out my lies in a second. He rests his chin on the curve of my shoulder, his lips ghosting over my skin almost teasingly.

"What are you doing home so early? Don't you still have another couple of hours?"

He inhales deeply, making me shiver.

"I'm off early today. Besides...I want to spend more time with you Flower...I've been far too busy for my preference."

The low rumble of his voice reverberates through his chest and into mine, and my cheeks redden as Aurora begins to purr at the sensation of his fingers touching the sliver of skin exposed by my sleeveless shirt rising up my belly.

"And I'm sure you've been feeling a bit lonely with me gone all day...I need to start making it up to you." He continues.

As much as I am enjoying his attention he's giving, Jessica's words worm their way back into my thoughts, interrupting my otherwise content mood...and Dakota picks up on it immediately, because he stops his playful affection.

"Something about that conversation with Jess must be bothering you Flower. What's wrong?"

I hesitate, biting my lip.

"Nothing..."

He turns me around to face him, his eyes soft as he gazes down at me, his hand brushing a lock of my hair from my eyes.

"Please don't lie to me Fleura, if something is troubling you I want to help...but I can't do that if you don't tell me."

I shift my feet, averting my eyes to the flip flops I'm wearing.

"Come here you."

His sigh is the only warning I get before I'm suddenly lifted off the ground, and my startled cry is swiftly followed by me wrapping my arms around his neck as he cradles me to his chest princess style while I'm toted up the stairs. I remain speechless as he sits us on the blue couch in our bedroom, with me sitting on his lap, his arms securely holding me here so I can't escape.

"Please Flower, you can tell me..." He murmurs, and he begins rubbing under my chin softly, the soothing action bringing up another purr of content.

~Tell him...he wants to help us...~

With Aurora's opinion clear, I sigh.

"I...I was talking to Jess the other day...and she brought up marking..." I mumble.

His eyes noticeably widen, and I fight the urge to hide behind my hair in embarrassment.

"What about that is worrying you?" His voice drops lower, more throaty than before.

Losing the battle, I let my hair fall in front of my face, creating a curtain as I look down. But it quickly disappears as Dakota's hands pull it back gently, at it takes a moment before I realize he's putting it up in a high ponytail with a hair tie he keeps on his wrist. He tilts my chin up to face him, a soft smile on his face.

"I really do love your eyes Flower...I wish you didn't hide them from me..."

Heat blooms across my cheeks and neck, and a soft growl slips from him when I bite my lip.

"She...she mentioned that she was surprised you hadn't marked me yet..."

I sound so pitiful, curled up in his lap like a child...

"Trust me sweetheart, I want to. So don't let that thought even cross your mind."

He presses a kiss to my temple before moving his lips to my ear.

"I've been wanting to mark you since the day I woke up on your couch..."

I shiver at his words, the feeling of his breath on my neck giving me goosebumps.

"Then why...?" I question shakily, and he sighs.

"Because marking does more than just leave a mark and create a mind-link...for she wolves, being marked will put them in heat...you do know what heat is right?"

The sudden realization sends my heart racing as I nod my head. Heat is what she wolves go through during a full moon if they haven't mated with their mate after finding them...it's a painful and extremely uncomfortable ordeal that only goes away after mating...but I had no idea why I didn't feel it the first full moon after meeting Dakota...until now.

It hasn't happened because Dakota has intentionally not marked me yet...I feel so foolish.

"As much as I would love to have my mark on you for everyone to see, I didn't want you to feel like you had to mate before you were ready, or have you suffer if you didn't...I want this to be on your terms Flower, there's no rush or time limit to this."

My heart flutters in my chest, touched by his patience and understanding. Because truthfully, as much as I'm not opposed to being with him that way...I don't think my confidence is there yet.

"Thank you...Dakota..."

He hums, tracing his thumb over my mouth.

"You don't need to thank me sweetheart...it's what mates are supposed to do."

He pauses, and his eyes glimmer as a slight smirk slants his mouth upwards.

"But...this doesn't mean marking is off the table completely...if you still want to..."

My blush returns as I tilt my head in confusion.

"You can mark me right now if you'd like..."

Aurora's automatic rumble of approval makes his smirk widen, and I have a feeling my eyes have turned gold from the way he's staring at them.

"I'll take that as a yes..."

He swiftly positions me so that I'm straddling his lap, and another sound comes from my chest that I wasn't expecting.

A lowly growl that catches me off guard, so much that I slap a hand over my mouth in response as Dakota chuckles.

"Don't be embarrassed Flower, I'm flattered to see this side of you."

He pulls my head closer, his mouth a fraction away from my own.

"Don't worry, your wolf knows what to do...let her lead."

~He's right, I can help you dear.~

My wolf immediately takes control, pressing my lips to his before slowly trailing down his chin, jaw and neck, hesitantly exploring his skin for the sensitive spot she was searching for. His hand runs up and down my back as he purrs, seeming to be content with letting us find the spot ourselves...and we do.

When we reach the curve of his neck and left shoulder, his body tenses as a growl rumbles out. We continue to kiss there experimentally, his hand tightening on my hip as he growls again.

With assurance we found the perfect place, my canines descend shortly before we sink them into Dakota's shoulder, the immediate rush of his thoughts into my head follows his groan, and the increase of my scent in the room as I feel he and his wolfs intense pleasure.

"Goddess Fleura..." he breathes out.

I retract my canines after a few more seconds, and then follow my instinct to clean the wound with my tongue, the puncture marks healing over immediately after.

Aurora gives me back control as I look up at him, his brown eyes now almost black. His hungry gaze sends my heart racing once more, and I honestly can't believe I just marked him without hesitation...where did that surge of confidence come from? From Aurora?

~Both of us dear, because we need to let every she wolf know that he is ours only.~

~She's right Flower, I'm only yours.~

I jump at Dakota's answering thought, I had forgotten he can hear my inner dialogue now.

"And until I mark you in return, this will let everyone know you are mine just as equally."

He removes his necklace from his neck and places it around mine, the pendant hanging to my stomach.

"That gamma pendant will tell everyone that you are my mate, so I want you to wear it for me...okay?"

I nod shyly and curl back against his chest, his amused chuckle is followed by a kiss to the top of my head.

"You're so cute when you're bashful."

We spend the next hour napping on the couch...until the sound of the washing machine going off wakes us up.

~~~~~~Hope you enjoyed! The chapter photo is what the mark will look like.

~~EIGHT~~

Hello my lovelies! I'm back! Hope you enjoy! The photo is what Dakota's ex looks like
~~~~~~

The next morning I woke up to an empty bed, the time on the clock saying 7:34 am and the warm sheets lets me know that Dakota just left, considering his Gamma duties start at 7:50. Despite knowing that I could see him anytime I wanted, I'm a bit disappointed that I didn't get to wake him up like I have been...

Sighing, I sit up and stretch before heading to the bathroom to do my usual morning routine. After washing my face and brushing out my wild hair, I go down stairs to the kitchen to find a covered plate with a note on top, my name written on the top with Dakota's heavy handwriting.

Fleura,

I didn't want to wake you because you looked so adorable as you slept, so I decided to just leave you breakfast here instead of waking you up.

Hope you enjoy, Flower.

A rosy color blooms on my cheeks as I uncovered the plate he made me, and the sight of a stack of blueberry banana pancakes with bacon and eggs makes my stomach rumble noisily. Smiling, I tentatively search our link to find him.

~Thank you Dakota...~

He responds immediately.

~You're quite welcome flower, tomorrow we are definitely eating breakfast together. I promise.~

I don't know how his voice can sound husky in a mind link, but it makes me shiver, even though what he said couldn't have been more innocent. My mind has really gone to the gutter since I've met Dakota...it worries me a bit.

Shaking my head, I take my plate to the dining room along with a bottle of syrup, but the smell of coffee distracts me. I don't remember...of course, Dakota made coffee for me too.

I fix my coffee and eat my breakfast quietly, contemplating what to do today. I finished the laundry yesterday, and I've practically dusted, vacuumed, mopped, and cleaned the entire house. I've already weeded the small garden behind the house and picked the ripe vegetables...and Dakota's pet turtle has a clean tank and has been fed.

The curse of being a house mate....eventually you run out of things to do while your mate is working. Even watching TV becomes boring after a while, especially when it's all reruns and scary movies that I refuse to watch alone.

I suppose I could always go out of the house for once...maybe look around the nearby town and window shop...or something...but I don't know it well enough to go alone...but Amy and Jessica are probably busy with their duties as Luna and Beta...Dakota's mom is busy with her three other pups, and to be honest I still don't know any other people here...

~Perhaps we should change that...~

Aurora murmurs in response to my thoughts, and I reluctantly agree. I'm the mate of this packs Gamma...I should do more than just hide in the house and feed Dakota...even though the latter is a challenge in itself with as much as he eats.

Making my decision, I wash up my dirty dishes and head upstairs to get dressed, taking a quick shower and shaving my legs before deciding on an outfit.

After some deliberation, I decide to finally wear the denim skirt I've had in my wardrobe for over a year but haven't worn once. The reason for that being that it stops just shy of the middle of my thighs, showing a lot of skin that I was never quite comfortable with...but, it's warm outside and it does look good on me...so I suppose I could try it. I pair it with a white off the shoulder top, the floral print fabric forming a little shawl that drapes over my chest and arms.

I slip on a pair of my favorite pink ballet flats and go to head out the door...but I stop to look at my reflection in the mirror first. Dakota's Gamma pendant swings a bit as I stop, and I touch a lock of my hair as I remember what he said yesterday...that he liked being able to see my eyes...

With that, I begin styling my hair, taking the front part that I usually hide my face behind and putting it in a crown braid, letting the rest hang down my back. It leaves my face completely exposed...and makes it impossible to hide behind a curtain of hair...

~Good...you don't need to hide your face...you are too beautiful to be hiding like that.~

My wolfs compliment sends me red faced again, which is plainly obvious with nothing covering my face.

~Our mate thinks that too, whether he says it out loud or not.~ She continues.

~Thank you...Aurora.~

~You don't have to thank me child, it is the truth. I've heard your mates thoughts through his wolf...he sees you as the most beautiful creature in existence. Don't forget that. Ever.~

Furiously blushing, I quickly head downstairs to the kitchen, putting tonight's dinner of ribs into two large crockpots before heading out the door with my purse in hand.

If I remember correctly, the pack house should be close by...not too far from the training grounds where Dakota is.

I make my way towards the pack house in silence, enjoying the scenery as I walk. As relaxing as it is though, I find myself getting a bit anxious as I get closer to my destination...and as soon as I catch sight of the large house I suddenly feel like turning around and going back home...

No...I've come this far, I'm not turning around now.

I argue with myself as I push forward, opening the front door and peeking in. I don't see anyone inside so far, but I can hear multiple heart beats on the upper floors and further inside the house....along with the sounds of fast moving feet.

I walk inside, but just as I'm five feet inside something collides into my legs hard enough to make me stumble back a step. After my heart calms back down and I regain my balance, I look down to see a little boy with curly blonde hair and soft brown eyes, which are tearing up as he stays on the ground. His lip quivering as he starts to cry...

His sniffles and hurt expression have me crouching down on the floor to comfort him, no doubt falling down on the wood floor has hurt him...whether it was his pride or his butt that was injured is the question.

"It's okay sweetheart, it's okay, don't cry." I murmur as I pull him into my arms, and he clutches my shirt tightly as he hides his face into my shoulder. I rub his back soothingly as his tears begin to subside, some of the stray ones dripping onto my skin.

"Noah? Noah? Where did you go sweetie?" A woman's voice calls out, which must belong to this little ones mother.

A dark haired woman comes around the corner, and she sighs in relief at the sight of me holding the pup.

"Thank you dear, I was so worried he had gotten himself hurt or lost." She says as she comes towards me, her hazel eyes curiously gazing at me as she does.

"He ran into my legs as I was coming in, and when he fell down he started to cry so...I figured holding him would help..." I explain a bit nervously, feeling guilty for making her child cry in the first place

"It's alright dear, unlike the rest of my little ones, Noah actually loves to be held. Though this is the first time he's enjoyed being held by a stranger..."

She reaches up to take him from me, but even though I try to return him to his mother, he clings to me tightly, seeming to prefer my hold instead of hers.

"Definitely a first...he seems to like you miss..."

"Fleura." I answer, and her eyes glimmer with recognition.

"You're Dakota's mate! It's lovely to meet you dear! No wonder he likes you!" She exclaims, and I'm a bit confused.

"What do you mean?" I ask.

"Well, little Noah tends to be picked on by the older kids, so it makes sense that he'd feel safe being held by you dear. I've heard that you are the sweetest thing!"

Noah nuzzles his cheek into my shoulder affectionately, and as flattered as I am, I'm still a little confused.

"Even though you're his mother?"

Her eyes widen a bit, then she chuckles.

"Oh no darling, he's not mine. Well, not biologically. He's one of the pack orphans, I'm just in charge of the house that they all stay in until they get adopted...or unfortunately age out."

I softly brush my fingers through his blonde curls, and Aurora's purr of content rumbles softly in my head....

"Since he's so attached to you, would you like spend some time with us? We're about to have breakfast."

I smile before nodding my head.

"I've already eaten, but I would love to help you if that's okay?"

"Absolutely! I would love some help! Trying to feed twelve energetic and cranky pups is a bit challenging sometimes."

I follow her into the kitchen, and proceed to help her while surrounded by a small pack of adorable but wild pups.

~~~~~

After everyone was fed and the youngest pups were taking naps, the woman who's name I learned was Tabitha, started heading back to her home...which happened only after I reluctantly handed Noah back to her, and considering that he fell asleep while sucking his thumb shortly after I fed him, he didn't protest in the slightest...even though my wolf did...

After watching him leave in Tabitha's arms, I try to take my mind off of the little sweetheart by exploring the rest of the pack house. Remembering faintly that Dakota said this was where Jacob and Jessica lived too, I try to make sure I don't invade on their privacy while I explore...

"Fleura? I thought that was you!"

I jump at the sound of Jessica calling my name, surprised by her sudden appearance downstairs.

"I didn't have anything to do at home...so I figured I'd explore a little..." I explain, and her wide grin splits her face to the point that I wonder if it hurts.

"That's perfect! I can give you the official tour! And you look so cute in that outfit, you have got to tell me where you got it!" She rattles off as she grabs my hand and begins showing me around the house, and I struggle to keep up with her near sprinting pace. She reminds me of the energizer bunny...or Taz from Looney Toons...

After showing me everything on all three of the other floors, she takes me up to the fourth which I know is the Alpha Suite...and she insists that it's perfectly fine for me to be here, it's only the Alpha bedroom I'm not allowed to go into without permission...which is perfectly fine by me.

As she's showing me the office, Alpha Jacob comes in.

"Hello Fleura...it's good to see you up here. Jessica has been wanting to show you around for a while."

I smile in response, still a bit nervous in his presence despite knowing he already views me as a sister...I suppose it's his powerful energy as Alpha that still unsettles me a bit.

"I also saw Dakota earlier, I'm happy to see you've marked him...he's quite proud of the mark you gave him."

I blush fiercely as Jessica squeals, bouncing up and down like she's spring loaded.

"Oh my Goddess! You didn't tell me that girl! I'm so happy for you!"

She squeezes me in a tight hug, and I struggle to breathe and worm my way out of her hold at the same time.

"Let her breathe baby, you're suffocating her." Jacob scolds lightly.

She lets go with a gasp and I catch my breath at last, a bit light headed.

"Tell me everything!" She almost begs as she grabs me by the shoulders.

"Maybe later baby, our guests are here for the meeting." Jacob reminds her, and I sigh in relief as Jessica's shoulders slump, silently thanking him for an escape from that conversation.

I wave bye as I exit the office, not wanting to intrude on private conversations. As I make my way down the stairs, I cross the paths of another Alpha male going up the stairs...and I'm so distracted by his intense energy and curious gaze that I don't notice someone else coming up the stairs until I collide with them.

"I'm s-sorry...I-I didn't mean..." I stutter out as I notice the woman in front of me.

"Why don't you watch where you're going you-?"

Her hard voice cuts off, her frigid blue eyes locked on the pendant around my neck. She looks at me almost accusingly...a bit of shock and anger in her expression.

"Where did you get that necklace bitch?"

~~NINE~~

"Did I stutter? Where did you get that necklace from?" The girl repeats, and I edge backwards as the she wolf almost stalks me down the stairs, her eyes livid as she holds my gaze.

"I...I..." I struggle for words, stress never helped me with conversation...especially not like this.

"Speak up brat, I don't have all day."

I feel my back hit the wall and gasp, realizing too late that I've just cornered myself between it and the angry blonde...this isn't good.

"My...my mate gave it to me..." Her eyes widen to the size of saucers, and the disbelief in them throws me for a minute.

"There is no way that a Gamma would be mated with someone like you...you're lying!"

Her words leave a painful sting, sounding all too familiar to the ones I heard as a kid...who knew they would still hurt me as an adult?

"But it's true...Dakota gave this to me yesterday..." I don't even sound like I believe it myself, so her doubtful stare shakes me even more.

"Please...you couldn't even please an Omega, what makes you think you could possibly satisfy a Gamma?"

Auroras soft growls in my head can't drown out the cruelty of her words ...why is she so angry with me?

"He's better suited with a strong she wolf instead...so why bother lying to yourself?"

My head drops as I close my eyes, and I curl my hand tightly around the pendant hanging from my neck...but the sudden sensation of being pulled somewhere else startles me.

Without even opening my eyes I can see a dark forest setting, the moon is barely a sliver in the sky as its dim light illuminates just enough for me to see...what is this place? I've never been here before...so why does it feel so familiar?

The snap of a twig turns my attention to my left, and the face that appears from the shadows surprises me. Dakota...what's he...where exactly...what is this?

My thoughts whirling, Dakota walks right by me as if I'm not even there...seeming to be searching for something I can't see. I turn to face where he's heading, and I'm shocked to see the girl here...but she doesn't seem to notice me either...Dakota lifts a hand to her face affectionately, the action leaving me shocked.

"Mate." He murmurs softly, and my heart stutters as I realize what this is...the girl was his first mate...the one who rejected him...

"I'm sorry...but no..." She replies, and a sense of dread fills my chest as I realize what's coming...and I can't do anything about it...only watch...

"I want to be a Luna...so anything less than an Alpha isn't good enough."

My heart feels like its twisting into a knot, and I can tell it's Dakota's heart I'm feeling even if I can't see his face clearly.

"I, Cassie Price, reject you as my mate."

Her voice is detached and emotionless, and she turns her back as I watch Dakota sink to his knees...the pain I feel in my chest almost bringing me to mine.

The setting in front of me fades to black as Cassie disappears, and as I blink my eyes open I look up to see the she wolf who broke my mates heart staring at me expectantly...like she just asked me the question.

"You definitely aren't fit to be his mate, that's why he hasn't even marked you yet."

That statement unleashes a flood of anger through me, and I'm a bit surprised when the growl in my head becomes one directly from my throat...but I hold on to it as I go from looking up at the heartless she wolf in fear to glaring at her in anger.

Just who does she think she is?

"Maybe I'm not...but you don't have a say in who is good enough for him!" My hostile reply startles her almost as much as it does me.

"Excuse me?!" She exclaims, and I step forward, staring her straight in the face despite her being taller.

"You rejected him because he wasn't the Alpha you wanted, because you didn't think he was good enough for you." I clutch the pendant a little tighter, feeling Aurora's confidence surging through me.

"You broke his heart out of selfishness...so you don't get to choose who he wants to be with, you don't get to decide who makes him happy again!!"

I continue, her obvious fury with hearing the truth not phasing me in the slightest.

"I may not be a powerful warrior...but whether or not Dakota wants me as his mate is his decision only. Whether you like it or not." I finish, and it's quiet enough to hear a pin drop in here, but with how violently she's shaking it won't be for long.

"You disgraceful little-"

She starts, raising her hand like she is about to hit me. But before she can swing, another hand flies out and grabs her tightly by the wrist, and as I look up to see who it is I notice the crowd who has no doubt been watching us...which includes Alpha Jacob and Luna Jessica...

"That's enough Cassie, I've heard more than I can tolerate from you."

It seems the young Alpha from the stairs is the one who stopped Cassie, and from the look on his face he is less than pleased.

"But...Liam-" She begins to protest.

"Quiet. I've put up with your behavior so far, but this is the final straw. One more word and I'm casting you out of my pack...am I clear?" Alpha Liam orders, with his pale blonde hair that's almost white, and his piercing blue eyes, he seems so familiar...but I can't put my finger on it...

"Well?" He asks when she stays quiet, and she reluctantly nods. He grunts before he turns his gaze to me, his expression softening automatically.

"I sincerely apologize Miss Fleura, I can promise you that this will never happen again." I nod, and he smiles a bit before turning to Cassie with a scowl on his face.

"Let's go."

He drags Cassie out a bit forcefully, only stopping to apologize to Jacob and Jessica before disappearing down the stairs. Jess quickly comes up to me, the reality of what just happened finally kicking in...making me feel a bit anxious and claustrophobic...

I need to get out of here. Now.

"That was the most amazing thing I've ever seen Fleura, I'm so proud of you. You told that girl off beautifully." Jess praises, and even though I'm happy for her compliment, I'm starting to feel a little overwhelmed.

"Fleura? Are you alright hon?" She questions as she notices my slightly panicked expression.

"I need...I need some air..." I gasp out shakily.

Her eyes widen as she nods in understanding, guiding me down the stairs and making sure no one gets between me and the back door. I silently thank her as I escape outside, breathing deeply in an effort to calm down.

Dakota

Anger. Stress. Panic.

It's those emotions flooding through my mates head that sends me from calmly patrolling the edge of the territory to flying towards the pack house at a breakneck pace...Zayev and I ready to rip apart the person making her feel that way.

I shift back as soon as I reach the yard, barely wasting time to pull on a pair of jeans before heading to the door...only to stop when it opens to reveal a familiar face...

Cassie...

The man pulling her out the door looks furious, and I can tell from his energy he's an Alpha. They both look up at me and stop, the young Alpha dropping his angry expression as the she wolf who rejected me gazes at me with conflicted eyes...lingering on the mark Fleura left on my shoulder.

"I apologize Gamma Dakota for how she treated your mate, I had no idea she would be so disrespectful."

A furious growl rumbles from my chest at his apology. She was the one who upset Fleura so much....that little...

"You. Did. What?" I growl out, and her eyes widen as she takes a step backwards, my less than friendly mood startling her.

"Dakota...I can explain..I-" She starts.

"I don't want to hear it. It's best you leave before I do something I regret." I go to walk into the pack house, but she grabs me by the arm.

"Dakota-"

I jerk my arm from her grasp, looking at her with disdain. Looking back on it now, I don't know why I ever desired to be with her in the first place. She's shallow and crude, with no respect for anyone's feelings but her own.

"I have nothing to say to you, except that I, Gamma Dakota Jackson, accept your rejection."

I continue in the house without looking back, intent on finding Fleura and make sure she's okay. I head up the stairs quickly, but with my little mate nowhere to be found I get more agitated...she was here the last time I felt her emotions...where did she go?

"Dakota?" Jessica calls out, and I turn to see her coming up the stairs.

"Where's Fleura? Is she alright?" I ask immediately.

"I wish you could've been here to see it, Fleura really told Cassie off. It shocked the hell out of all of us..."

I blink in surprise, trying to imagine my sweet Fleura being confrontational...and not quite imagining it. It's not that I don't think she can stand up for herself...it's just I haven't seen anything other than her shy side...

"I suppose you'd have to see it to believe it." She realizes, letting her thoughts run through my head and replaying the events I just missed...and as much as I found myself proud of her ferocity over me...something she said doesn't sit right with me...

Why on earth would she agree that she isn't good enough for me?

"Where did she go?" I question.

"When she saw that we were watching, she got really anxious, so I helped her outside to get some fresh air..."

I go back down stairs in a flash, following her scent out the back door since her thoughts are hidden from me. After a few minutes I find her sitting on the pier that sits over the large pond on the territory, holding her shoes as her feet slowly swish back and forth in the water.

I stay quiet as I get closer, noticing how deep in thought she is. What's going through her head?

"Flower?" I call out, and she jumps at my voice.

"Dakota?" She exclaims, pressing her hand over her heart in surprise. I kneel down next to her quietly, taking her face in my hands softly as I look her over...relieved to see she hasn't been crying and is otherwise calm.

"I guess you heard what happened..." She murmurs, placing a hand over one of mine.

"Felt it actually...are you okay?" I ask, and she nods in response, to which I sigh in relief. Now on to an equally pressing matter...

"I want you to know right now that you should never feel like you don't deserve to be my mate...that you aren't good enough for me."

Her eyes widen, but before she can argue with me I capture her mouth with mine, letting my restraint lessen as our kiss deepens...her soft gasps and sighs increasing as I continue, and her attempts to keep up with my gentle assault only encourages me.

If anything...she's too good for me...and my goddess I plan on proving it to her. No matter how long it takes.

"Dakota..." She sighs against my mouth, shivering as my hands move down to trail up her back, tracing the warm skin curiously.

But reluctantly, I pull away from her before I let myself get too carried away...I don't think she's quite ready for that yet...although I don't plan on holding back so much now that I know she's comfortable with this.

I chuckle as she instinctively tries to follow my retreating mouth, enjoying the view of her flushed cheeks and darkened eyes...so beautiful.

She truly has no idea how much power she has over me...that there isn't a thing I wouldn't do for her...

"You don't have to be a warrior to be my equal, because you're already perfect for me..." I continue, pressing a kiss to her forehead before looking back into her eyes, trying to keep the image of her biting her lip from distracting me.

"So don't let anyone try to tell you different, okay Flower?"

She nods again, and surprises me by pressing a quick kiss to my cheek...her own getting impossibly redder in response as I smile like an utter fool...

Goddess, she's going to be the death of me...

Grabbing her shoes and purse, I scoop her up in my arms, her squeak of surprise adorable as she wraps her arms over my shoulders.

"Come on, let's go home. I think you've had enough action for one day."

~~TEN~~

Fleura

I can do this...

I try to convince myself as I pace back and forth in the master bathroom, my thoughts a bit scattered as I attempt to figure out the best way to approach a particular subject with Dakota.

It's been a week since Dakota and I had that heart to heart at the pond, and things have gotten much more intimate between us. He kisses me on the mouth more, and much more heated than the pecks he used to give me. He lets his hands wander more when we get caught in a particularly heated kiss, and he's been leaving hickies in the place where he wants to mark me.

He always stops before it goes too far though, but I can tell he wants to go further...to be as close to me as mates possibly can be to each other...and truthfully, so do I. I want to be closer to him, I want to complete our mate bond and bear his mark on my shoulder, to make sure that everyone knows we're mates.

But...that requires bringing up the subject of...mating.

Goddess, just the word makes me blush, how in the world am I gonna ask Dakota about this out loud if I can't even think it to myself without turning red faced and bashful? And what is even the best way to bring this up? Do people just ask when they want to mate? Is there a specific way of asking? Or do they just know?

~You could always let me take the direct approach...it worked well the last time I had control...~ Aurora murmurs, and as much as she is right...I can't do that this time.

~No...I want to be able to do this myself, I can't always have you take control when I don't know what to do...~

She stays quiet after my reply, but I can tell that she understands. Her helping me mark Dakota was a one time thing, but mating is something I'll have to be able to handle myself...especially considering that even with my limited knowledge on it, I know it's going to happen more than once between mates...

A shiver runs down my spine, no doubt caused by the cool air of the bathroom hitting my wet skin, the shower I had taken was what got me thinking about this in the first place...

~You don't need to stress about this so much dear, this isn't a test. He is our mate, there isn't a wrong way to ask about mating...~

I sigh. ~I suppose you're right...~

~Of course I am dear.~

I pout irritably, cheeky wolf.

"Flower? I'm home! Where are you?" I jump at the sound of Dakota's voice traveling through the house, and my hands instinctively hold the towel I'm wrapped in tighter around me.

I can do this...just go for it...

I chant to myself, and Dakota's footsteps get closer.

"Flower?" He calls out again.

"In here!" I reply a bit loudly, exiting the bathroom to go to the bedroom door. But I only get halfway there before Dakota comes in, his eyes turning dark at the sight of me as he forgets whatever he was about to say, his low growl sending my heart into an erratic rhythm. We stare at each other for what seems like an eternity before he clears his throat, pulling his eyes from me with some effort.

"I'll just wait outside until-" He starts, beginning to turn around and exit the door. My eyes widen as I quickly run up to him, knowing that if he shuts that door I would lose all of the courage I spent so long building up. I stop him by grabbing the back of his shirt, my forehead resting against his back.

"You...you don't have to go..." I mumble with red cheeks, embarrassed at how it sounds coming out of my mouth.

"Flower?" I barely notice the surprise in his voice as I mull over what to do now, my wolfs advice of just going for it now seeming like a bad idea...I have no idea how to go through with this.

~For the love of the goddess girl, say it! You've got his attention, tell him what you want!~

~It's not that simple for me! I've never done this before, what am I supposed to do? Ask him if he wants to mate?~

~I would personally go for the 'telling then kissing' approach, but I suppose that works too.~

My face must be a violent shade of red right now, goddess I'm pitiful...

"You know I can hear your thoughts, right Flower?" Dakota murmurs, and I look up in shock to see him staring down at me, his eyes dark and hungry looking as his mouth curls into a soft smile...

I think I've forgotten how to breathe.

"Sweetheart, I'm all yours. So if you want me, all you have to do...is ask..." I shiver at the feeling of his mouth brushing against my ear, his voice a husky whisper.

"Well flower?" I nod to answer his question, and he turns my chin towards him as he presses his lips to mine, softly moving them with mine as he pulls the hair tie out of my dry hair, letting it fall down my shoulders as he slowly backs me up to our bed...that I promptly fall on when the back of my legs hit it.

He quickly joins me after he yanks off his shirt, and I let my fingers hesitantly trace over the defined muscles of his stomach as he hovers over me and begins pressing kisses to my jaw and down my neck, the sparks where we touch almost addictive, his soft growls mixing with my increasing pants as he moves down to my collar bone.

But the feeling of the towel being pulled from my chest has me tensing up, and when it falls off completely I instinctively cover myself with my arms as I feel Dakota's eyes on me, my own eyes turning away out of embarrassment...I've never felt this exposed before...

"Please don't hide yourself from me Sihu, I want to see every beautiful inch of you..." Dakota whispers as he recaptures my lips, and his gentle touch seems to melt away my insecurities, causing my arms to go limp as he pulls them away from my body.

"Let me show you just how beautiful you are..."

Liam

Leaning back in my chair, I rub a hand over my eyes, trying to rub some of the tiredness out of them. Late night paperwork has never been a perk of the Alpha title...especially when it's the kind that's required when the Alpha title changes hands...I honestly don't know how dad did it, but I'm definitely going to have to learn.

Remembering that I have a meeting to schedule with the construction company about the new home being built on the territory, I grab my phone and unlock it...but my intention to go straight to the calendar app is interrupted by the last thing I was looking at before I put the phone down...

Fleura Stratton.

She looks so familiar...how do I know this girl?

I think to myself as I stare at the photo on the screen, the ice blonde hair and different colored eyes of the she wolf mated to Gamma Dakota of Starry Creek has been a reoccurring thought since the day I met her.

Fleura seemed to feel the same way, for I noticed her inquisitive looks both before and after that dreadful she wolf Cassie harassed her...and my initial reaction to both protect her and apologize for the rank chasing mutt's behavior felt almost instinctive...like it was my job...

Which is why after I sent Cassie packing I had a talk with Alpha Jacob about her, and found myself intrigued by her particular story.

From what Alpha Jacob told me, Fleura is 25 years old and was a former gypsy wolf that lived in Minnesota, she had spent most of her life alone and wasn't accustomed well with pack life because of it. She met Dakota in the woods when he was injured by a group of hunters that were chasing her for sport...she had dragged him to the safety of her home to tend his injury, and after he recovered and found out they were mates, they moved to his pack in Missouri.

However, as interesting as her story is, it brings up more questions than answers. I don't have any idea how I could recognize a girl who grew up in Minnesota when I've spent my entire life in Iowa, and considering that her childhood memories are fuzzy, I doubt she'll have any memories of me either...

So why does it feel like I know her?

It's that plaguing question that had me scrambling for a reason to ask Alpha Jacob for a picture of her, which ended up being that it was to see if any of the packs up north recognized her...to see if she had any relatives. Which was a truthful reason, I have used it for that exact purpose since I've returned to my pack here in Iowa...but outside of a few wolves recognizing her from her time as an adult gypsy wolf...I've gotten nothing but frustration out of it.

Who is she?

Sighing, I put my phone down to go get something to eat from the kitchen, my wolf's nagging for food is not the kind of headache I want right now. So, after I quickly raid the fridge for some leftover pizza, I head back up to the office...only to find my dad sitting at his old spot at my desk.

"Hey Dad, I was just about to call you..." I trail off when I realize he isn't listening. In fact, it seems like he doesn't even know I'm here.

"Dad?" I repeat, and as I get closer I notice that he's staring down at his hands, holding my phone with Fleura's picture open on the screen.

"Liam....where did you get this picture?" He finally speaks, his voice sounding far away...like his mind is somewhere else completely.

"I met her at the Starry Creek pack down in Missouri...she's mated to Gamma Dakota. I felt like I knew her from somewhere, so I asked the

Alpha if I could have a photo to use for possibly finding anyone who knows her..." I explain, and I can see the look of utter disbelief in his eyes.

"What...what is her name?" He asks almost hesitantly.

"Fleura Stratton, she's 25 years old...Dad, what's going on? Do you know her or something?" I ask, genuinely worried for him. It's not like him to be so...so caught off guard.

"Remember...Do you remember that story I told you about me? The one from when I was your age now?" He starts, his voice raw with emotion. I pull a chair up beside him, ready to listen to what's so heavy on his mind.

"Yeah, I remember...it was about your first mate...the one before mom." I recall, he told me about his first mate a couple of years ago, a woman named Saraphina who he had lost to an enemy pack.

He nods, running a hand over his mouth. "Well...there was a part to that story I didn't tell you..."

"And...what part was that?" I question, trying to figure what could be so bad about that untold part that he left it out of the story completely.

"...the day I lost Saraphina...was also the day I lost my child...the child I had with my first mate..." He continues, and the anguish in his eyes tells me that this isn't a joke in the slightest....

Dad had a kid before me? I'm not his first kid?

"A daughter...her name was Skye."

~~ELEVEN~~

I'm back my loves! I dropped you on a cliffhanger, I know! But here's the next piece of the puzzle !!!~~~~~~

Ian

Goddess this can't be real...

I stare at my sons phone screen in silent awe, pausing from my explanation to try and wrap my head around just the thought of my daughter...being alive. That my three year old baby girl that I lost is now a grown woman, shes been alive for the past twenty two years and I missed them all...

"Dad? You were saying?" Liam asks, his words concerned while the rest of his mind must be a whirlwind of emotions...but what else can I honestly expect considering I just told him he has an older sister?

"Sorry...her name was Skye. She was my first child with a young witch named Saraphina." I start, my mind already going back to her face...the elegance in how she moved, the way she seemed to know exactly what I was thinking...

"I was a younger man then...just turned seventeen when I met her, and she was nineteen...and more mature than me in a few ways." I chuckle, trying to remember exactly what made a sweet and nurturing woman like her fall for a rebellious rascal like myself. Maybe it was the fact that she saw the good in everything...

"As mates usually do, I fell hard and fell fast. Her light brown hair and green eyes seemed to cast a spell on me...no pun intended, and it wasn't long before I moved in with her...choosing to leave my pack land to be with her."

I look up to see my son giving me a surprised look, obvious curiosity in his eyes. I can't blame him, I never told him how rebellious I was when I was his age...along with other things.

"Why would you leave the pack land? Weren't you in line to be Alpha?" He asks, and I sigh...I suppose this was bound to be told one way or the other...

"I was a rebellious teenager then...instead of wanting the Alpha position, I dreaded it. I wanted to be free to live my own life and do what I wanted instead of being chained to desk duties and pack politics...at least back then anyway. My older sister, your aunt, had more interest in being Alpha than I did at the time, so I decided to leave home under the pretense of looking for my mate so she could start her training to be Alpha...but I never expected to actually find Saraphina while I was off galavanting and, according to my father, shirking my responsibilities." I explain, mentally shaking my head at my old self.

"So...what changed?" He asks, and I look down to the phone once more before taking a deep breath.

"Everything." My wolf whimpers as the memories begin filling my head.

"Three months after meeting Saraphina, she found out we were expecting our first child...and I was so terrified but so excited about it...my first pup...I had no idea what to do, so I called my parents. They were so excited by the news of their first grandchild...but they had unfortunate news to share..." I pause.

"Which was?"

"A good portion of the pack members had broken away from the pack, deciding that they wanted to rule the pack themselves instead of bowing to the current alphas...my parents. The groups defection had sent the pack into a bit of a panic...and they warned me to be careful and look out for my family."

I still remember how insistent my mother was to come home, only to have dad say that considering I'm already off the territory, to stay away for a little while and lay low until the traitors were dealt with for good...and after a year and a half of doing exactly that and seeing nothing more than a few menial attacks that lead to easy defeat...we thought it was over, so my parents came down to see their granddaughter more often as time passed...

"But after Skye turned three, we dropped our guard...we put those wolves behind us. And one night I decided to leave Saraphina and Skye home when I went up to the pack land for a quick visit with my dad...and it's a decision I've regretted every day since..."

My hands begin to shake so bad I nearly drop the phone to the floor, but Liam catches it and grabs my hand.

"About two hours after I left, I felt an immense pain coming from my mark...and my wolf immediately had me flying back home at a breakneck pace. But when I got there, it was too late...I found carnage outside the house...fallen wolves laying lifeless in the snow...and Saraphina...goddess Saraphina..."

The image of her is burned painfully into my memory, the sight of her beautiful face covered in her blood, her body ravaged by unforgiving teeth and claws...her once shimmering emerald eyes vacant and empty...it brought me to my knees in agony. And as I prayed to the goddess that it was just a dream...a sick nightmare that I'd wake up from with a cold sweat and a racing heart...my wolf reminded me of who was missing...

"Then the realization sank in...that Skye was missing...I started searching for any sign of her frantically...following her faint scent until I found her spilt blood...and another dead wolf...but she was nowhere to be found...her scent disappeared into thin air..." My chest squeezes painfully at the memory, my heart beginning to twist like it did then...and I try to get through the rest of the story before it breaks all over again.

"I searched for her desperately along with my father and the pack, days on end...and those days turned to weeks, weeks turned to months...and those months turned into one year...and then two..." I sigh, "but with each day without finding her the others started to lose hope...slowly dwindling down until it was just me and dad, who was trying to get me to come to terms with the fact that Skye was gone and never coming back. To stop running myself ragged when it was probably hopeless...but I couldn't...she was my baby girl, I didn't want to stop."

I take a shaky breath, failing to keep a couple of tears from escaping the corners of my eyes.

"But even though I believed that I would know if Skye was gone, after two years of tireless searching...I was burned out...I had nothing left in me. So after six more months of searching...I finally accepted she was gone...and it was the hardest thing I've ever done."

"Dad..." Liam starts, but he doesn't seem to know what to say.

"I went back to the pack...with your aunt finding her mate in a Beta from another pack, it was now me who would become Alpha...and six months after I came home...I saw your mother again for the first time since I left the pack...and it shocked the hell out of me when I found out she was my second chance mate..."

Kelly and I had known each other since we were young pups...and had been friends before I left the pack...but I never expected to find her as my mate.

"It was complicated at the beginning...I was still grieving and struggling to fill the role as Alpha...but your mom understood. She knew I needed time...so she just tried to be there for me in any way she could...and helped me when I needed it the most. And as time passed we got closer...then a year after I found out she was my mate, we had you..."

Liam's face has a blank look to it, but I can feel his emotions rolling turbulently under the surface.

"I can see why you didn't tell me this...not just because it still hurt to remember...but also because you didn't want me to feel like mom and I were replacements..." His voice cracks a little, and I immediately place a hand on his shoulder.

"You never were a replacement...you and Skye are two different people...the void that was left in my heart after she and Saraphina left my life is still there, but my heart grew bigger to love both of you just as much." I explain, pulling him into a tight hug.

"...Do you think...do you think Fleura could really be Skye?" He asks quietly after a moment, and we pull out of our awkward embrace. I stare at the photo still glowing on the phone screen, and I can feel myself reaching out to cling to that shred of hope once again...and as much as I know how badly this could end if she isn't my daughter...I can't just sit here and not know for sure...if there is a sliver of hope that she's my little girl, I need to take it.

"There is a definite possibility...there's too much of a resemblance to ignore. The same hair, the right age...those exact same eyes...heterochromia is rare in wolves. But to have exactly the same color in the exact same eyes...it's too much of a coincidence." I admit...and Liam nods.

"I'll see if I can clear out my schedule so we can go together...I'll give Alpha Jacob a call to let him know we'll be coming back down to Missouri soon." He says with a weak smile.

"Going back? You just came back from there a week ago...why do you need to go back?" We both freeze at the sound of Kelly's voice, and I turn to see my red haired mate standing in the doorway, her curious expression a sign that she hadn't heard me talk to Liam. I sigh and take Liam's phone from his desk, getting up to walk towards her.

"Liam found this girl in Starry Creek...and I need to see her for myself..." I say as I hand her the device.

"Why would you..." She trails off as she glances down at the picture, her eyes widening as she covers her mouth in shock.

"I know it's a long shot...but she looks too much like her to ignore. I fully understand that this can end badly for me...but I need to take that chance-" I explain, only to have her cut me off by pressing a finger to my mouth.

"I understand darling...it's okay. You don't have to explain it to me." She replies softly, "I know that this is important for you...just as I know that if I was the one in this position, I would go too..." She strokes my cheek affectionately, and I sigh.

"This is your pup that we are talking about, I'm not going to get in the way of that...but I am going with you." My eyes widen at her words, and she smiles up at me.

"This is going to impact your life significantly sweetheart...so I'm going to be there with you. Besides, if she really is your daughter, I want the chance to meet her myself."

I never cease to be amazed by how understanding she is...how she always looks out for me without a second thought or hesitation.

"Thank you dear...you have no idea how much this means to me."

I pull her into a tight embrace, letting her warmth and scent relax me and settle my turbulent emotions. Having her there will definitely help me face all this...especially considering I have no idea how this meeting is going to go.

"You're welcome darling...I know you would do the same thing for me..."

As Liam makes his plans and clears his schedule, I can feel my wolf pace anxiously in my chaotic mind...both of us nervous and slightly terrified of what's to come when we see Fleura in person. And I begin praying to the goddess that she really is who I believe she is...that she'll finally let me hold my daughter in my arms like I prayed for all those years ago.

~~TWELVE~~

Dakota

This must be what heaven feels like...

I think to myself as I stare at my beautiful mate, sleeping soundly with her cheek pressed against my heart as her hair spills onto my chest...her body soft and warm as she lays on top of me. Her sweet scent fills all of the air around me, making me purr in utter content as I curl a strand of her hair around my finger.

Her bold approach last night caught me off guard to say the least, her internal debate over how to ask me about mating was both surprising...and adorably sexy considering the circumstances...but now she's all mine...and I'm all hers, our mate bond is complete and we're connected in every way possible...I couldn't be any happier in this moment.

Fleura's soft sighs perk my attention, and I smile down at her face as she slowly wakes up from her dreaming...that adorable scrunched up face of hers making me chuckle as she fights against waking up.

"Flower...time to wake up baby." I murmur as I trace my thumb over her cheek, and after a moment of her face scrunching up her eyes flutter open, her sleepy expression slightly filled by confusion.

"Morning baby." I murmur.

"Dakota...you're still here? Don't you have to work?" She mumbles back, a crease forming between her narrowed brows.

"I figured after last night, I would spend the day with you...what do you say?" I reply, and her confused expression turns to one of surprise and embarrassment, her face turning red as she recalls last nights events.

"Oh..." She squeaks out, and as I chuckle at her innocent reaction she tries to escape from my reach, but I gently trap her underneath me with her back pressed to the bed.

"Don't run from me Sihu, I love seeing your adorable expressions." I whisper in her ear, unable to fight a smile as it causes her to shiver in response. Her slight gasp as I nip her ear makes her bite her bottom lip, and I growl lowly at the sight of it.

"And I especially love when you bite your lip like that...it makes me want to kiss it." I admit huskily, and her eyes widen shortly before I kiss her just as she lets her bottom lip go, her body relaxing from its tense state as she starts kissing back, both of us purring as we enjoy each other's touch...her hands tentatively sliding up my chest and behind my head, tangling in my hair.

Goddess she's perfect...

"Now that you've calmed down...what do you want to do today?" I murmur after I pull away, pressing a kiss to her neck.

"You really took today off?" She questions, and I smile.

"Mmhm...so I could spend it with you, doing whatever you want." I reply, and her soft blush makes me chuckle.

"Anything I want? Are you sure?" She questions.

"Of course, you're my mate Flower, a day of spoiling you is exactly what I want to do. I've been so busy lately that it's left you by yourself during the day...I want to change that." I explain, brushing a stray lock of her hair from her face as she shyly averts her gaze.

"So what would you like to do first?" I ask after a moment of silence, and just as she narrows her eyes in deep thought, her stomach and mine rumble noisily, and I chuckle as they make the choice for us.

"How about we take a shower, and then I take you somewhere special for breakfast?" I suggest, and her answering smile has me purring.

"That sounds perfect..." She murmurs, and I let her get off the bed and watch as she crosses our bedroom in fascination, content with just waiting for her to finish her shower before I take mine. But as she reaches the bathroom door she stops, turning to peek at me over her shoulder with red cheeks.

"Aren't...aren't you going to join me?" She asks shyly, and I struggle to keep myself seated.

"Do you want me too?"

"I would love for you too...Ohpitsa." She replies, and for a split second I'm speechless.

"What...what did you say? Say it again." I rush the words out when I get my thoughts in order, and her face turns even redder.

"O-Ohpitsa...." She stammers out, and I waste no time before moving in front of her, pressing my mouth to hers in a deep and passionate kiss that takes her by surprise. That word, so small but meaning so much seems to ignite an even stronger spark in me.

Ohpitsa...the Apache word for sweetheart.

"I-I take it that I said it right?" She pants out as I move down to her jaw, trailing down her neck with a satisfied purr.

"Yes you did...and feel free to call me that whenever you want." I murmur against her skin before pressing a kiss to her shoulder, and her back arches at the sensation of me touching the mark I gave her last night.

"What...what was that?" She pants out, and I let out a low growl before I kiss her mark again.

"My mark flower...you seem to be quite sensitive there..." I slightly tease as she trembles again, and I guide her in front of the bathroom mirror to show it to her, the red heart design intermingled with a black infinity symbol. I circle my arms around her waist and rest my chin on her opposite shoulder as she touches the mark in awe, both of us admiring its reflection.

"It's beautiful..." She murmurs, and I couldn't agree more.

"It definitely is, flower. But as much as I would love to admire it and you all day, if we don't hurry up we'll be eating lunch instead of breakfast." I remind her reluctantly, and she giggles as she pulls me towards our shower.

~~~~~~~~~~~~~~~~~

After our shower, we got dressed and headed to town for a late breakfast of waffles and eggs at a restaurant I love for it's home style cooking.

After that, I convinced her to go clothing shopping after I caught her staring at some of the window displays with obvious interest, and I have to admit that it was quite enjoyable watching her show me all the outfits she tried on, and how her cheeks turned red every time I complimented her on how beautiful she looked. I learned very quickly the difference between the ones she didn't like period, and the ones she liked but didn't think she looked good in, having my link with her helping me understand her inner thoughts much more in depth than just reading her expressions.

The sound of her hesitant thoughts snap me back to the present, and I can hear her edging to the entrance of the dressing room to show me the last outfit she's trying on before I pay for everything and we go to our lunch...or early dinner considering the time.

"Flower? Are you alright?" I call out to her curiously, and she sighs.

"Yes...I'm just not sure about this one..." She trails off, and I smile.

"Well come out and let me see."

She steps out after a moment, a conflicted expression on her face as she twists the loose end of one of the French braided pigtails I gave her this morning, the braided parts ending at the base of her skull as the rest is tied into two ponytails. But that's not what draws my attention the most...

The white dress with yellow sunflower print leaves me a bit speechless, it's short ruffled sleeves and hem that ends just above her knees makes her look adorable...swishing over the denim capris that stop below her knee, the white sandals she liked showing her pink toenails still pristine from the spa day she had with the girls a few days ago.

"Well...what do you think?" She asks after I do nothing but stare, and I blink a few times.

"It's perfect Fleura, you look lovely." I answer as I step towards her, placing a hand under her chin to rub it, making her quietly purr as her cheeks flush and she leans into my touch instinctively.

"You say that a lot..." She murmurs.

"Because I mean it, and I'm going to keep saying it long after you start believing it too...my little sunflower."

I press a soft kiss to her lips, but our moment is interrupted when a soft 'aww' comes from beside us. I look up to see one of the store employees staring at us with obvious adoration, and I can feel Fleura fight the urge to hide her face in my chest out of embarrassment.

"I'm sorry, it's just you two are the sweetest couple I've ever seen...you remind me of me and my husband back when we were your age." The older woman says apologetically, a bit teary eyed.

"It's okay...thank you." My mate squeaks out before darting back to the dressing room to change.

"Don't let that one go honey, I can tell you two are meant for each other."

I smile at her words, being more accurate than she realizes.

"Oh, trust me, I don't plan on letting her go."

Fleura walks out of the dressing room just as I say it, wearing her original outfit of one of my burgundy tank tops with her black one underneath, along with her denim shorts and flip flops.

"Ready to go flower?" I ask as I take the stack of clothes in her arms, the rejected ones already put back. She nods, and I proceed to start paying for everything she picked out...despite her argument that it was too much.

"You're going to have to get used to me spoiling you too, Flower...because I'm going to keep doing that as well."

She doesn't say anything, just stands there while I listen to her wolf argue with her internally as I pay and grab the large bags before engulfing her hand with mine.

"Come on baby, lets go get something to eat."

~~~~~~~~~~~~~~~~~~~~

We had initially planned to go to a movie after our meal, but Jake called me to unfortunately tell me that we had a last minute meeting with an Alpha pair from another state. Fleura insisted that I didn't need to apologize for cutting our day short, that my Gamma duties were too important to ignore, and we could always see a movie anytime we wanted.

When we returned to the pack house, I asked if she would like to join me to the meeting, figuring that even though she probably would say no due to the presence of high ranking strangers, I would ask anyway. Just like the Luna and Beta Female, being mated to me means she has a rank equal to mine.

But, as I predicted, she declined, though she did seem flattered that I wanted her to join me. So after giving her a kiss, I left her downstairs to go the Alpha's office, the meeting itself lasting much longer then I expected it to. Time slipped by a little faster for the others as they caught up, while I spent it sneaking conversation with my mate waiting downstairs.

After it finally ends two hours later, I quickly return to the first floor.

"Now that I'm finished, would you like to go home and watch a movie? I can make grilled cheese sandwiches and popcorn to go with it." I offer, and a wide smile stretches across her face as I pull her up from the couch.

"That sounds-" She starts, but the sound of small footsteps moving fast catches our attention, as does the sound of excited giggling which makes her turn her head with excited eyes. I turn to follow her line of sight to see a small pup running towards us, his blonde curls bobbing as he heads straight to my mate.

"Hello Noah! How's my little buddy?"

She bends down a bit to look at him, and he reaches up to her with his hands close to her face.

"Up! Up!" He calls to her, and without hesitation she picks him up in his arms, her soft purr of content piking my curiosity. I always thought she'd be good with pups, but watching her hold him in her arms as he plays with her hair seems almost...natural.

~She and her wolf have bonded with the pup...she wants him as her own.~ My wolf responds, the realization clicking as I continue to watch them interact.

When the little ones brown eyes flicker to my face, he becomes silent as he stares at me...a mixture of curiosity and apprehension.

"Won't you say Hi, Noah? He's friendly, I promise." She encourages, and follow her words by holding out my hand for him, his little nose sniffing it cautiously before grabbing my fingers in his tiny hands. His strong grip surprises me since he can barely wrap his hands around my fingers, but I find myself feeling very proud of it.

"Tiny hands, my only weakness..." I murmur, glancing at Fleura as she giggles with a soft blush, "you've got quite a grip there little man, what's your secret?"

"Wolf man!" He giggles, and I can feel my smile widen as I stare down at him, my wolf encouraging me to continue playing with the pup...which is exactly what I want.

"Oh really? Well little wolf man, can you growl?" I ask, and he grins.

"Grrrrr!" He growls out, and have to admit that it's pretty cute.

"That was pretty good, what about a howl?"

"Awwwooooo!" He cries out loudly, both me and Fleura laughing as it echoes through the house.

"You guys are so cute together!" A woman's voice calls out, and I turn to see the familiar face of Tabitha staring at us with a happy smile.

"Hello Tabitha." Fleura murmurs.

"Hello dear, I see Noah has attached himself to you again." She answers with a chuckle.

Again?

"Noah first met your mate a week ago, it took getting him to fall asleep to finally pry him off of her." Tabitha explains after noticing my confusion.

"Well I hate to cut this short, but it's bed time for the little ones." She explains after a moment, but as she goes to take Noah from my mate, he immediately latches onto my mate even tighter.

"No." He whines, hiding his face into Fleura's neck.

"Come on kiddo, you can see her tomorrow."

"No, I wanna stay." He continues, and I can see a similar look of reluctance on my mates face as well as his.

"I know sweetheart, but you need to go home with Ms. Tabitha." Fleura tries to console him.

"No, mama. Stay with mama."

It goes quiet, and all of us feel the shock at what he just said, Fleura's reaction is just as instinctive and possessive as mine.

~Our pup.~

~~THIRTEEN~~

Fleura

That moment was probably the most surprising of my life...or at least, it ranked high on the list. Sitting high up there with finding Dakota, and then discovering he's my mate...

Anyway...after little Noah's plea to stay with me, and calling me mama, it didn't take much discussion between me and Dakota before deciding to actually adopt him. I knew that I had grown very attached to little Noah in a short amount of time...but I wasn't sure how to ask Dakota about making him ours...thinking that he would probably want biological children first...

But seeing that soft look on his face as he played with the little pup in my arms warmed my heart, and it surprised me how he grew attached faster than I did. But I guess I should've known that from the start, because as serious and stoic as Dakota is when he's working, it goes away the second he comes home to me.

"What are you thinking about so hard flower?"

Dakota's voice startles me from my thoughts, and I look up to see him grinning at me from his place on the ladder, different shades of blue paint smeared on his old t shirt and hands from painting the bedroom that will belong to Noah once the paperwork is processed. The walls being painted light blue with white clouds that I've painted on, slowly darkening as it reaches the navy blue ceiling that Dakota is covering with glow in the dark stars, the dome shaped light looking like a moon when it's cut on...

It's perfect.

"I was just thinking about Noah...I'm a bit nervous..." I admit, and he immediately comes down from the ladder to stand in front of me, his can of navy paint still in hand.

"Why are you nervous love?" He questions, raising an empty hand to cup my cheek, and I lean into it.

"It's just...I've never been a parent, Noah is going to be my first kid...what if I do something wrong?"

"Flower, it's going to be okay...Noah's going to be my first too, so we can figure it out together, and I did help my mom take care of my sisters when they were little...so I do have some experience. Besides, my mom has raised four pups including me, so if there is anyone we can ask for help, it's going to be her. She's going to be thrilled about being a grandma, and my sisters are going to adore being aunts."

I feel the anxiety fade at his words, and as I look up to meet his gaze, I notice a smear of blue paint dried on his chin, and I can't help but giggle at the sight of it.

"What's so funny sunflower?"

I giggle again, "You have a little bit of paint right there." He chuckles as I poke his chin.

"So do you love..." He trails off as he leans in closer to my face, and my cheeks tinge pink.

"Where?" I ask, and his grin widens.

"Right...there!"

I jump at the feeling of cold paint being smeared over my cheek, and as Dakota laughs with his brush in hand, I decide to return the favor and dab some white paint on his forehead...and then a full scale fight erupts between us. Both of us careful not to splatter any on the walls as we chase each other around the room, trying not to slip on the plastic covering the carpet as we try to tag each other in any place possible. Clothes, skin, and even hair is targeted as we laugh at how ridiculous we're being...like children, but I love it...and I think he does too.

"Come here you!" He calls out as he chases me, the tables turning after he decided to dip both his hands in blue paint and run after me, and I struggle to keep out of his grasp while laughing, knowing that he'll catch me regardless.

"Gotcha!" He announces triumphantly after I accidentally corner myself in the closet, pinned against the wall whose paint is actually dry. I try to find a way to squeeze past him, but each exit route is blocked by one of his paint covered hands...I'm trapped.

"No, no, no! Dakota don't!" I protest with a squeal and laugh, shutting my eyes as I prepare to be covered with paint.

"What fun would that be?" He murmurs, sounding like he's right in front of me, and just as I open my eyes to confirm it, his mouth presses to mine in a deep kiss...to which I close my eyes again as I stand on my tiptoes to circle my arms around his neck...

I should've known better, because the second I let my guard down, I feel his hands grab my butt, no doubt leaving two handprints on the back of my khaki shorts.

"Dakota!" I cry out in surprise after pulling away a bit, and he laughs victoriously before lifting me off the ground, and I immediately wrap my legs around his waist to keep from falling...clinging to him with a squeak of surprise.

"Yes flower?" He asks, looking at me with a smug expression and a devious twinkle in his eyes.

"You got paint on my shorts! I'll never be able to get those handprints off!" I scold with a beet red face, and he only smirks wider.

"Good...that way when you wear them, everyone will know you're all mine..." He replies, giving me a playful squeeze that makes me squeak again. Goddess this man makes me blush, all this excitement can't be good for my heart.

He begins walking out of the closet, and noticing my confusion, he grins.

"I think it's time we cleaned up Flower, don't you think?" He purrs, and I can already tell from the hungry look in his eyes that cleaning up won't be the only thing we'll be doing in the shower this time...not that I'm complaining in the slightest.

"That sounds like fun..." I answer a little more confidently than I expected, and his answering purr is immediately followed by him kicking the bathroom door closed with his foot.

------A few days later----

"Where's Noah?" I call out to the pup, who is trying his best not to giggle as we play hide and seek in the house. I already know exactly where he's hiding, but I figured I draw it out so it would be more fun.

It's been a couple of days since Noah officially became a member of our family...I love that word by the way...family. And he seems to be adjusting well, already having explored most of the house with me. He especially loved his bedroom, and it made me really happy to see that wide grin on his face when I said it was all his, no doubt he didn't have his own room in the home he was living in. He couldn't decide what to go to first...

The little rocket shaped toy box filled with both the few new toys I bought him and the ones he already had, the bean bag chair that looked like Earth, the bed fitted with space themed bed sheets, or the giant teddy bear sitting in the corner that mema, as he's come to call Dakota's mom, gave him as a present. But needless to say he investigated it all, and was especially fond of the glow in the dark stars on the ceiling.

"Noah..." I call out again, smiling broadly as I hear him giggling from upstairs, and I slowly begin to creep up the stairs to the game room that Dakota's been redoing. Turning it from just a place to watch movies and play video games, to a play area for Noah...and other future pups. Having already put in things like a little table for him to sit and color at, pillows and a miniature cabinet filled with coloring supplies. Dakota decided to leave his turtle tank upstairs, and Noah loves to watch the little creature occasionally.

Creeping up the stairs, I peek over the edge to see his little tuft of blonde curls sticking up from behind the cabinet, and I grin as I slowly tiptoe towards him.

"Boo!" I call out as I lean over the top, and he jumps before bursting into a fit of giggles that's extremely infectious, leaving us both laughing as I scoop him up in my arms.

"Again! Again!" He cries out excitedly, but as much as I would love to fulfill his wish to play again, there is something else we have to do first.

"Maybe in a little while baby, but not right now." I answer, and his responding pout almost makes me change my mind.

"Why not?" He asks, but before I can answer, his tummy answers for me with a loud rumble of hunger, as does mine.

"I thought we could have lunch first, how does that sound?" I offer, and he bobs his head excitedly.

Once we reach the kitchen, I help him wash his hands and put on his bib before sitting him in his hook on high chair attached to the island countertop and preparing his lunch, consisting of some leftover grilled chicken we had last night for dinner cut into bite sized pieces, some soft cooked baby carrots, and his favorite cup of apple sauce with his small spoon. As he starts going to town on the chicken and carrots I set on his tray, I refill his sippy cup with water.

~Hello flower, how's our little man doing?~ Dakota ask through our link, and I grin as I hand Noah his cup, giving my mate a look at him just as he shoves a handful of chicken in his mouth with bits of carrot smeared on his chin.

~I'd say he's loving the food, don't you say?~ I answer, and my smile widens as he chuckles at the sight.

~That's my boy.~ He says with amused pride, and a wave of warmth spreads through me, much like the one I felt when Noah called Dakota 'daddy' just yesterday, the look on Dakota's face was so awestruck and happy...it literally made his day...and mine too.

~Are you going to be joining us for lunch today?~ I ask hopefully, though I have the feeling that since he isn't here already, he won't be joining us.

~No, unfortunately...my shift won't end for a couple more hours, sorry flower.~

I sigh externally as I watch Noah's messy attempt at eating applesauce, making me grin a bit.

~It's alright Ohpitsa, we'll be waiting for you.~

~You know I love it when you call me that...~ He purrs before his link disappears, and I sigh as I wet a wash cloth to wipe off my sons face and hands, him giggling at the sensation until I stop to wipe off his tray. Removing his bib, I sit on the stool beside him to eat my lunch.

"Where's daddy?" He asks curiously, and I smile at him.

"He's working sweetie, but he'll be home in a little while, I promise." I answer with a poke to his nose, and he giggles before going back to sipping his water.

"Can we go see him?"

I shake my head with a disappointment, and he pouts a little.

"Not this time, but I think we can surprise him tomorrow instead, what do you think?" I offer, and he bobs his head excitedly.

"Come on sweetie, I think your favorite show is about to come on." I say after I drop my empty plate in the sink, the time reminding me that Paw Patrol is about to start.

Just as I get into the living room and cut the show on, the doorbell rings. Hitting pause, I head to the door with Noah on my hip, him playing with a piece of my hair. Opening the door, one of the three people on the other side surprises me.

"Alpha Liam...what are you doing here?"

~~FOURTEEN~~

The picture is what Fleura's mom looked like Enjoy the chapter!~~~~~~

Ian

I'm not sure what's leaving me speechless the most, the fact that she looks even more like Saraphina than she did in the photo, or if it's the little boy that she's holding on her hip, his blonde curls not too different than the ones of the she wolf he's attached too. My heart squeezes painfully at the thought of potentially missing out on both my daughters life...and the birth of a grandson.

"Fleura, it's good to see you again." Liam greets, he too eying the toddler as Kelly squeezes my hand in reassurance.

"You too, Alpha Liam." She replies, and her soft voice restirs my memory.

"Please, just Liam is fine. And who's this little man? I don't think we met last time I was here."

"Oh, this is Noah, my son...me and Dakota recently adopted him." She explains, and I find myself both relieved I didn't miss a birth, and saddened that I missed the adoption.

"It's nice to meet you little guy, how old are you?" He asks, but the pup remains silent as he looks at us with hesitation in his brown eyes.

"He's eighteen months old, sorry...he's a bit shy." Fleura explains with a sigh, and I feel my heart race a little as she looks at me and my mate curiously...a bit of a shy blush painting her cheeks.

"Oh, Fleura, these are my parents..., Ian and Kelly Anderson." Liam introduces us, and I hold my breath as she shakes my mates hand, and then reaches for mine.

"It's nice to meet you Mr. Anderson..."

"Please, call me...Ian." I reply, having to fight the serious urge to say Dad instead. I don't know for sure yet, so I can't say that.

"And Kelly for me dear." My mate adds.

Fleura smiles, and little Noah pulls on her T-shirt to get her attention, and she turns her gaze back to him before looking back up to us.

"Would you like to come inside and sit down? Noah wants to watch his show."

"Of course, thank you." Kelly nods, and we enter the house. Fleura shows us a sitting area near the kitchen while she sets up Noah in the living room, a kids show playing on the TV as he watches intently and chews on a giraffe shaped teething toy Fleura got out of the freezer.

"Um, can I get you anything to drink?" She offers, and we shake our heads.

"So...what brings you back here?" She questions as she sits down in a nearby armchair.

"Well, I initially had business with Alpha Jacob, to make up for the meeting we didn't get to have the last time we were here...because of Cassie..." Liam explains, and I look at him in surprise. I knew that she wolf had been a nuisance for Liam, but I had no idea she was here the last time he was.

"Oh, right." She murmurs, looking a bit strained.

"And since I was here, I decided I'd come down and apologize again for her behavior towards you that day."

"What behavior Liam? I didn't hear anything about this." I ask, and he looks towards me with a slightly tense expression.

"Well, Cassie had followed me here despite me telling her not to, and just as the meeting started I came down to see Cassie being disrespectful to Fleura...but she was quite impressive with telling the girl off before I had to step in." He explains, and I can feel my blood boil under my skin. Kelly squeezes my hand again, which helps me calm down immensely. Though I'm still angry with the disrespectful pup that's so attached to my son.

"What exactly caused the event in the first place?" Kelly asks curiously.

"Well...she was Dakota's first mate...but she immediately rejected him. She was upset that I was with him now..." Fleura trails off, and I raise an eyebrow.

"First mate?" I ask.

"I...I'm Dakota's second chance mate, and he's my first." Fleura blushes, and the pieces click into place.

~Just like I was for you sweetheart, what are the odds of that?~ Kelly murmurs through our link.

"Is this him?" She asks, and I look at the picture she's pointing at. It holds an image of Fleura standing next to a much taller man, him kissing her temple as she's laughing with a blush on her cheeks. He has to be Gamma Dakota, even though I haven't officially met him yet...I have a feeling that'll change soon, I want to meet the man myself.

"Yes it is..." Fleura says with even redder cheeks than before, her hand going to her shoulder instinctively to touch the mark I can faintly see there.

"You two are such a cute couple, I can already tell you just adore each other...and that he's quite sweet on you." My mate swoons, and the girl goes to playing with her hair like she wants to hide behind it...something Skye used to do whenever she was embarrassed. The longer I sit with her, the more it feels like her...

"He is..." Fleura almost whispers.

"Alright mom, that's enough of that, you're embarrassing the girl." Liam half scolds, and Kelly apologizes as she puts the picture down.

"Turtle!" A little voice calls out from just below us, and I look down to see Noah reaching for the stuffed turtle that fell out of my mates purse. The toy used to be Skye's favorite, and it's one thing of hers that I've held onto all these years...even though it has long lost her scent.

He picks it up in his little hands, and with his wide eyes and blonde curls...it's like seeing my memory play out in real life all over again.

"Baby, that's not yours, give it to mommy please." Fleura calls to home, looking at us apologetically. "I'm sorry, he loves turtles, so he got excited..."

"It's quite alright, Fleura." I assure, feeling a bit nostalgic again.

"Come here sweetheart." Fleura murmurs, and Noah toddles over to her a bit reluctantly so she can pull him into her lap.

"You have to ask first before you play with other people's toys, oka-" She cuts off as her hand touches the stuffed animal, and I swear my heart stops beating altogether as I watch her eyes go from blue and green...to gray. The last time I saw happen was with Saraphina...whenever she got visions of the past...which means...

"Mama?" Noah calls out, reaching up to her face which is frozen like a statue, her eyes gazing out to the unknown. But she doesn't respond, she doesn't even twitch...which worries all of us, especially me. I get up to sit down on the stool in front of her, placing a hand on her skirt covered knee.

"Fleura? Can you hear me kiddo?" I ask softly, and when she still doesn't respond I reach a hand up to her cheek. "Bunny?" I call again, and this time her eyes flutter rapidly, and I sigh in relief as her normal eye colors return.

"What...what did you call me?" She whispers dazedly, and I swallow hard. The nickname I gave Skye had rolled off my tongue on instinct, it had felt like the right thing to say.

"Bunny...I called you bunny." I answer, and her breath hitches in her throat, which makes my wolf whimper in response.

"Why does that sound familiar? Why do I feel like I should know you?" Her voice wavers, a stray tear sliding down her cheek, as I wipe it away her body freezes, and she grabs my wrist so quickly that it makes me jump.

"I do know you..." She murmurs in realization, and just as my heart begins to race with excitement her eyes squeeze shut, her pained expression disappearing as her head lowers to her lap.

"Mama?" Noah says again, but Fleura remains silent as we all stare in worry.

Fleura

It was so unexpected.

When I had touched the stuffed turtle Noah was holding, my fingers running over a place on its belly where it had obviously been stitched back together, it was like the day I met Cassie all over again. I immediately felt I was being pulled somewhere else, but to much different place than before...a place that felt familiar to me...somehow...

Instead of a dimly lit forest, it was a bright and sunny backyard full of colorful flowers and a small gazebo...I can almost feel the warmth of the sun and the soft breeze, almost smell the flowers and fresh cut grass...tugging on my mind like an old memory...

"Daddy!!! Daddy!!" A young voice cries out, it too sounds familiar. When I turn to face where it's coming from, my eyes widen, not believing what I'm seeing...

It's me...a much younger me...tears streaming down my face as my younger self runs past the gazebo and to the back porch of the house...to another face that shocks me.

"What's wrong bunny? Why are you crying?" A much younger Ian asks, looking so much like Liam I have to do a double take.

Wait a minute...did younger me just call him 'daddy'?

"Brandon was mean to me again! And this time he ripped up Shelly!!" Little Me sniffles, and I gasp as I see her raise the same turtle from before, this time with its belly ripped open with stuffing coming out.

"He did? Let me see." Ian replies with both shock and a bit of anger, taking the toy in his hands carefully.

"I've had just about enough of that boy, I'll need to have a talk with his father." He mutters irritably, only to have his expression soften when he hears little me sniffle again.

"Don't cry bunny, Shelly will be okay, I can fix him." He murmurs soothingly as he wipes away the tears.

"You can?" She says with a hiccup.

"Yeah, mommy's probably better at this, but I can fix him for you. Stay right here."

He gets up and disappears into the house, coming out a moments later with a sewing box in his other hand.

"Come here." He says as he sits in the porch swing, and she immediately climbs up to, wiggling her way onto his lap.

I watch as he lets the little girl pick out a thread color from the box, which was orange, struggle to thread the needle after multiple attempts, and then carefully if not perfectly sew up the hole in the toy.

"There you go, all better now." He grins triumphantly as she takes the toy and squeezes it to her chest.

"Thank you daddy! It's perfect!"

"You're welcome Bunny. Now, lets go see Brandon's father and have a little talk." He smiles as he stands up with her in his arms, walking past the gazebo and disappearing from my sight.

As the scene around me begins to disappear, I hear someone calling out to me, and as I return to the present I feel a hand press to my cheek...which brings my eyes back into focus to see Ian in front of me.

"Bunny?" He calls to me, and my eyes flutter in surprise.

"What...what did you call me?" I whisper dazedly, part of me wondering if I'm still having the vision.

"Bunny...I called you bunny." He answers, and my breath hitches in my throat. This is real...

"Why does that sound familiar? Why do I feel like I should know you?" My voice wavers, a stray tear sliding down my cheek out of some unknown sadness. As he wipes it away my body stills, recognizing the sensation, and I grab his wrist so quickly that it makes him jump.

"I do know you..." I murmur in realization, and almost immediately afterwards a splitting pain fills my head, making me squeeze my eyes shut and curl my head towards my lap, the sound of Noah's voice sounding distant as an onslaught of images fills my head along with the pain...

~~FIFTEEN~~

A bove is what Fleura's father Ian looks like, Hope you enjoy!

It's too much...like a dam has burst in my head that I didn't know existed.

Memories of Ian, raising me alongside a woman named Saraphina. It was obvious that they are my real parents, all those moments we spent coloring together, eating together, playing hide and seek with Dad and tending the garden with mom...Dad being the tickle monster as he chased me and Mama around the house, both of them cleaning me up when I scraped my knees...

It all feels so familiar...but at the same time like it happened to someone else...like it was someone else's life. For the longest time I considered the older woman named Maya my mother...but she never was...

But how...why did she raise me to my teenage years? The gap between my happy family and living with Maya is like a black hole...one I suddenly find myself being pulled into.

It was cold...snow covered the ground and swirled in the air, making our house look like one of Mama's snow globes. Daddy had left for the day, promising to be back to help me build a snowman like we did every time it snowed...

So me and Mama bundled up to make snow angels and have a snowball fight, taking breaks from the cold by going inside and drinking hot cocoa with cinnamon and giant marshmallows, not to mention using some of the snow to make snow cream.

We were having so much fun laughing and playing in the snow...that is, until we heard growling in the woods. At first I thought it was daddy...but Mama's scared face made it clear that it wasn't, especially when all those big, scary looking wolves started coming towards us.

"Run Skye...go to the house right now..." She told me in scared voice, and I hesitated as her hands began to glow.

"Run! Now!" She orders desperately, and I clutch Shelly to my chest as I make a mad dash to the backyard, going as fast as my little legs would take me.

The growls get louder as they mix with crashing noises and animal cries of pain, but just as I reach the backyard a pained scream fills the air...and I look back to see mama has disappeared inside the huddle of wolves, the air filled with nothing but silence.

"Mama?" I call to her weakly, my heart racing in my chest. I take a step forward only to freeze at the sound of a growl...much closer than the ones before. I slowly look up to see a large gray wolf staring down at me, baring his teeth with a growl, his muzzle painted red.

With wide eyes I realize he's standing between me and the house...my safe place is now out of reach. So I do the only thing I can think of:

Run.

I sprint towards the woods, darting side to side within seconds of the beast snapping at me. I weave my way through the trees to try and get away, at one point going through the narrow gap of two that the wolf temporarily gets stuck in.

Just as I look back to see how close he is, I trip over a large tree root and fall on my stomach. I get up as quickly as possible...only to come face to face with wolf again as I do, his large paw raking across my face before I can react.

It hurts...I cry out as I'm sent flying into the base of a tree, my turtle lost as I curl into a ball and cover my eyes...the pain making me whimper as both tears and another warm liquid runs down my face, blurring my vision as I tremble. I hear the heavy footsteps and growling of the beast...but I'm too scared to look up, I just cry and beg for daddy to help me...to protect me like he always does.

He doesn't...and just I feel the wolf loom over me, his harsh growl right in my ear, something flies over me and hits him hard, his startled whine followed by the sound of wolves fighting. I keep my eyes squeezed shut as flying snow hits me, not daring to peek even after it goes quiet after a cut off whine fills the forest.

After what feels like hours, something comes towards me...and I curl into a tighter trembling ball as they stop in front of me.

"Little one? Are you okay?" A woman's voice calls as the scent of rogue fills my nose, and I open my eyes to look up at the blurred silhouette hopefully.

"Ma-mama?" I whisper hoarsely, and the woman sighs.

"I'm so sorry little one...but I couldn't...I was too late..." She murmurs as she kneels down, and my sobs echo painfully loud as the reality hits me. She reaches towards me, and I instinctively flinch away from her hand.

"It's okay sweetie, I promise I won't hurt you..." She murmurs, and between the grief, the cold, and the pain...I don't have it in me to fight against her offered comfort.

She turns my head towards her, her brown eyes filled with horror as she looks at my face. She immediately rips off a piece of her shirt and presses it against the hurt area gently, and I shiver as some of the snow begins to melt inside my coat.

"Come here little one." She carefully picks me up, and I go limp as she cradles me in her arms, the she wolfs warmth cocooning me like mama's used too...for a moment I pretend it's her as I close my eyes, the last thing I hear before the darkness pulls me in is the strangers voice.

"I promise to protect you little one, no matter what."

....

"Fleura? Fleura baby? Can you hear me sweetheart?"

Dakota's voice cuts through the empty silence, as well as the cries of my little boy calling for me as he tugs on my shirt. I blink my eyes as my vision returns again, looking up to see my mate in front of me, his panicked expression relaxing a bit as I meet his brown eyes. Noah stretches his little hands up to my tear soaked face, his own cheeks wet from crying.

"Baby?" Dakota murmurs, and I hiccup as the memories hit me all over again, the sobs that rack my body spur my mate into action.

"D-Dakota..." I hiccup as he pulls my face into his chest, his hand cupping the back of my head as Noah clings to me and sobs into my shoulder.

"It's okay Flower, it's okay...I'm right here, everything is going to be okay." He murmurs soothingly as he rubs my back and strokes my hair at the same time, and I let all my sadness dampen his shirt as he holds me close.

Dakota

I sigh in relief as both my mate and my son finally cry themselves out, tucking both of them under the covers of our bed as Noah clings to her tightly in his sleep.

Brushing a strand of her hair behind her ear, I kiss her temple before standing up to leave the room, shutting the door gently behind me and then leaning my back against it. I run my hands over my face as the images that played through my mates head replay in mine once again, turning into an invisible bystander as I watched the happy life she had be shattered in a heartbreaking moment...

No four year old should have to go through that...to see that kind of horror. It's more than likely the reason her memories were so fuzzy, her minds defense against that hurting her again was to have her forget...who wouldn't want to?

Pulling myself together, I head downstairs to the room full of people. The young Alpha Liam sits on the couch in silence, his blank expression hiding a great deal of shock and confusion while his father Alpha Ian stands in the window with his head hung low as the woman I assume is his second chance mate attempts to comfort him.

I'm currently in the presence of my mates father, stepmother, and half brother...all of which are processing things very differently at the moment. I'm not sure exactly what to say right now, but I have to say something...at least someone has to. Looking down at the floor, I see the stuffed turtle that was in my lap, and I pick it up before taking a deep breath.

"Alpha Ian?"

He turns to me slowly, his face filled with both grief and anguish. Both Luna Kelly and Alpha Liam look at me too, and I go to sit down in the chair my mate was sitting in earlier, the rest of them following suit.

"To be truthful...I honestly don't know what to say to any of you right now. Considering the things I saw in Fleura's head...and her current emotional state, I'm not sure I'm going to know for a while..." I start, and it stays silent.

"All I do know right now is that you're her family, and you need some answers...and right now I can only give you three."

Ian looks at me, anxious for my answers.

"One...Fleura remembers you...she knows you're her father...and that your first mate was her mother."

Kelly squeezes his hand as he nods, telling me to keep going.

"Two, she remembers the attack...but she didn't see what happened to her mother." I leave out the part that she heard her mothers dying scream...he doesn't need to know that, me and Fleura having that ingrained in our memory is more than enough.

"Thank the Goddess..." He murmurs.

"And three...the rogue she wolf that saved her life...Maya, if I remember correctly, was the one who raised her. I can only assume that she didn't know you were alive...and that she believed moving Fleura would keep her safe."

As they process that I sigh, knowing the next thing I'm going to say is going to be difficult to hear.

"What I don't know is how she is going to handle all of this later...or how long it's going to be before she even wants to. She just got the biggest bombshell of a lifetime dropped on her, and after twenty one years of not remembering...she has a mother to grieve for. And I know from experience that she needs to have this time...even if it means she does it alone..."

Fleura's dad sinks his head into his hands, and remind myself to keep it together. Fleura needs me...as does Noah.

"I'm not saying you have to leave the territory, just...she needs time, and space to process everything. We can't rush her through this...no matter how much we want her to feel better."

Everyone nods after a moment, still silent. I may not know everything Fleura is experiencing, but I do understand the loss of a parent. I was fifteen years old when my father was killed in a rogue attack...and even though I had to keep it together for my distraught mother and my infant sisters, I still mourned him.

"I wish we could have met under different circumstances...but it is good to meet my mates family. Perhaps once things settle down we can talk and get to know each other." I say as I stand up, and the rest follow.

"Of course...we'll stay close by...and thank you Dakota, I'm glad my daughter has you in her life...she needs you now more than ever." Ian murmurs as he shakes my hand, all of them filing out the door slowly as I watch. Once the door shuts behind them I collapse back into the chair, closing my eyes as I allow myself process all the emotions swirling in my head...allowing myself a brief moment of instability and uncertainty.

Because once I get out of this chair, I'm going to be the one who holds it together for all of us.

~~SIXTEEN~~

After having a few hours to sit and pull myself together, I got up and finished the normal routine for the day. Noah woke up around the time I finished dinner, which consisted of hot dogs and french fries...though he just got a cut up hot dog and some of the left over green beans in the fridge I heated up for him.

I had hoped Fleura would join us...but I decided to let her rest and come down when she was ready. So after we both finished with dinner, I gave Noah his bath and helped him get ready for bed...after a little convincing and a bed time story, he slept in his bed instead of with Fleura. And after I cleaned up in the kitchen, I joined my mate in our bed...a little disappointed to see she hadn't even gotten up to change into her pajamas. I just pulled her close to my chest and slept beside her, hoping that I could provide her some comfort.

Getting up this morning, I start the routine again at 8 am...part of me knowing that my mate wouldn't be feeling up to it. I had already told Jake that I would need a little time to be with Fleura and Noah while this sorts out...and he told me to take my time and that Beta Paul would cover for me in my absence.

After taking my shower and getting dressed, I head down stairs with the laundry baskets and put a load of color clothes into the washer...remembering both the teachings of my mother and Fleura's instructions for her clothes. Colors, whites, jeans, and towels are separated and washed accordingly, as are bedsheets. Colors in cold water, whites in hot water, and always pretreat stains before washing. Some of her clothes are air dry only, and others only machine dried on the low setting.

Once that is started, I go back upstairs to wake up Noah, only to find him awake and playing with a few of his toys on the floor.

"Morning little man." I call softly, and he looks up at me with a big smile.

"Daddy!" He replies, and after a moment of letting him stand up by himself, I crouch down to his level to meet him as he waddles towards me.

"How about we get us some breakfast kiddo?"

He bobs his head enthusiastically at my suggestion, making me chuckle as I reach out and scoop him up in my arms, ruffling his blonde curls as Zayev rumbles happily.

"What do you want to eat this morning?" I ask as we head out his room and down the stairs, and his brown eyes sparkle excitedly.

"Pancakes!" He says, and I chuckle.

"I think I can do pancakes, but only if you help me...you think you can do that?"

He bobs his head enthusiastically again, and I worry for a second that it will come flying off. Once we get into the kitchen I help him wash his hands before sitting him on the kitchen island, and he watches intently as I take out everything from bowls and hand mixers to the pancake mix and eggs.

Looking around the kitchen, I find a few things that could definitely taste good.

"Would you like some chocolate chips in yours little man?" I ask, and he grins.

"Yeah!"

"That sounds awesome, what kind do you think mommy will like?" I continue as I show him a few ingredients I put on the counter. After a moment of looking with his lips pursed out, something Fleura does that he's already starting to imitate, he points towards a bag of brown sugar.

"That one!"

"Good choice, I think she'll love it."

I immediately begin pouring ingredients into bowls, one small one for Noah's chocolate chips, and a bigger one for me and Fleura's brown sugar and cinnamon. I help Noah crack the eggs and assist him in mixing his bowl, both of us laughing while making a little bit of a mess as we stir, and once I get both mixed up well enough, I decide to let my boy have a try.

"Alright buddy, how about you sit right here and keep stirring your bowl while I go wake up mommy?" I ask as I sit him in his chair and set the spill proof bowl in front of him, letting him grab on to our smallest mixer and go back at it.

"Okay daddy..."

I grin and head back upstairs, and I sigh as I see Fleura still hasn't moved out of bed yet.

"Flower?" I call softly, sitting on the edge of the bed and brushing the hair out of her face.

"Come on sweetheart, time to wake up..." I whisper as I lean down to her ear, and she whimpers a little before her eyes lull open, and I'm relieved to see that they aren't as bloodshot as they were yesterday.

"Dakota..." She murmurs groggily, and I press a kiss to her temple.

"Morning Flower...how'd you sleep?"

"Okay...I guess." She replies while stifling a yawn, the sadness in her expression clearly stating that her newly recovered memories are still heavy on her mind and heart.

"I know you still feel bad sweetheart, but I can't let you stay in this bed any longer. Besides, you didn't eat dinner last night...so me and Noah are making you some breakfast." I murmur as I brush my thumb across her cheek, and her eyes glimmer a little bit at our pups name.

"Come on Flower." I say as I stand up, taking her hands in mine and pulling a little. After a second she lets me pull her upright, and after she stands up she immediately wraps her arms around me in a hug, her face hidden in my chest.

"How about you take a nice warm shower, change into something more comfy, and then come downstairs and eat some breakfast?"

She nods, and I sigh before I lean down and press a kiss to the middle of her forehead. And I wait until she finally unwraps herself from my arms and goes into the bathroom before I go back downstairs, my smile returning as I see my son stirring away...a little bit of a mess in front of him.

"How's it going Noah?" I call out, and he giggles.

"All done!!!" He says happily, and I can tell from the batter on his face he's already tried some of it. I quickly take the bowl and mixer from him and look at the contents, glad most of it is still there.

"Good job buddy. Now I'll make the pancakes...right after I clean you up a little."

I wet a wash cloth and gently wipe off his face and hands, as well as wiping off the counter and fixing his sippy cup full of milk before I get to cooking. Making Noah's silver dollar pancakes first and setting them aside to cool down a little before he eats them, he'll burn his hands and mouth otherwise.

As I start on the brown sugar and cinnamon ones, I keep an ear on the running shower upstairs, as well as keep tabs on Fleura's thoughts through the link...or try to. Either her mind is unusually quiet, even for her, or she's shutting me out again...something that she typically does when she's feeling overwhelmed with emotion. Personally that worries me...I don't know how to help her if I don't know how she's feeling.

Before I finish the rest of the food, I cut up some peach slices and give them to Noah along with his cooled pancakes, and he digs in happily after I put his bib on. I go back to cooking afterwards, and just as I finish the last one I hear my mate come downstairs. I look up to see her entering the kitchen, her hair damp and pulled up in a messy bun, wearing one of my college t shirts and her cotton pajama shorts.

She looks refreshed, and if I'm not mistaken, like she feels a little better. And if that's the case I'm happy...it's means I'm actually helping her. She looks up to catch my eye, flashing me a soft smile that makes me sigh in relief.

Definitely helping.

"Look whose joined us for breakfast kiddo." I point out, and Noah turns to look at Fleura with the biggest smile on his face, which is covered with little smears of chocolate.

"Mommy!" He calls out excitedly, and she grins at his messy face before pressing a kiss to the top of his head.

"What have my sweet boys been up to?" She chuckles.

"I helped daddy make breakfast!"

"Did you now? And what's for breakfast?"

"Pancakes!" He exclaims with a grin, holding out one of his silver dollar ones to her in a sweet offer. She chuckles and takes a bite of it, making Noah giggle.

"They're yummy, thank you baby." She says after she eats it, and then comes up to me.

"And thank you too Ohpitsa..." She murmurs softly, cupping my face in her hands as she stretches up on her tiptoes. I grab one of her hands and kiss the palm, happy to see a tinge of red on her cheeks.

"Of course Flower, you don't have to thank me. I'd do anything to make you happy." I whisper back, and after a moment we both make our plates and eat, enjoying each other's presence as we do.

Fleura

It's been a couple of weeks since that morning, and Dakota's been nothing but supportive and understanding. He's spent a lot more time at home, helping me around the house with chores, playing with our son who just loves spending time with his daddy, and cooking meals...goddess the man can cook, I can't honestly decide what was better- the broccoli and cheese soup or the teriyaki chicken and shrimp veggie stir fry.

But I suppose the best thing he's done is just talk to me...or listen when I did, about how he understood to some extent what I was going through, about how hard it is to lose a parent. I can't begin to count how many nights we sat on the couch, whether it was spent talking about my struggles with both my memories and my identity...or just me curling up in his lap with my mind link wide open to him, so he can know my inner thoughts on nights I don't even want to talk about them.

As for my identity...I'm still struggling with knowing who I really am. Fleura Stratton, or Skye Anderson. The former feels like a lie...while the latter feels like a stranger...an entirely different person. I honestly don't know who I am anymore...but I guess the only thing I can do is figure out who I am now, instead of trying to be who I was then.

Which is why a week ago, with Dakota and Noah by my side, I reconnected with my father, and the rest of my lost family.

It was a little tense at first, but the second he pulled me into a hug, feeling the familiar sense of love and safety in his embrace, it felt less like Ian...and more like Dad. I think both of us cried again that day, but more out of happiness than grief. Especially when I introduced Noah to Ian by calling him his Grandpa...to which Noah immediately responded with calling him Granpaw.

Meeting Liam again as my brother was a new kind of joy, though with the way he acted it's a little hard to grasp that I'm his older sister. He's so mature for his age, even as an Alpha...and now an uncle, which made him immensely excited.

As for Kelly, my father's second chance mate, it wasn't as awkward as I expected. I don't see her as a replacement for mom...but she makes my dad happy, so I still consider her family...I'm sure once we get to know each other more we'll get closer.

As of now though, I've convinced Dakota to go back to preforming his Gamma duties, he's spent enough time away as it is...besides, even though it still saddens me to think about my mother, it's not as overwhelming as it was at first. There are some things I still need to figure out, but I have plenty of time for that...being surrounded by all of my family and my friends helps immensely.

Which is why I'm spending time with both my father, brother and my friends Jessica and Amy in the the living room of the pack house, my son running around as he chases after some of the pack members children.

"It's good to see you out and about Fleura, we were all worried about you." Jessica says as she sits down next to me on the couch, and I smile as I watch Noah go giggling after an older girl he's playing with.

"Thank you, it's good to be out again. I feel better than I did a while ago..." I answer, and appreciatively take the glass of sweet tea she hands me, honestly feeling a little warm.

"I'm glad, you look like you feel better. I remember how rough last week was when I came to visit." She continues, and I nod as I take a few sips. Why do I feel so warm when the air conditioning is blasting in here?

After a few minutes I've already drank all of the tea, and with no relief I decide to get some more. But as I stand the room begins to swirl around me, and the last thing I hear before I black out it the sound of the glass shattering as it hits the floor, and people calling my name.

~~SEVENTEEN~~

The first thing I notice upon waking up is how my head hurts, the pain throbbing in my temples like bongo drums...

What happened?

My ears catch the sounds of muted voices, and a soft beeping noise coming from further away. But I'm more focused on the feeling of someone holding my hand, the warm sparks letting me know it's Dakota.

I finally pry my eyes open to see harsh lights above me, which makes me groan as it only intensifies my headache.

"Fleura? Sweetheart?" My mates voice calls softly, and his worried face appears above me...thankfully blocking out the bright lights.

"Dakota? What's going on? Where am I?" I murmur, and he he sighs in obvious relief.

"I brought you to the pack doctor, you really scared me Flower..." He explains, and my eyebrows furrow in confusion.

"Why? What happened?" I ask, my memory a bit fuzzy. I slowly sit up despite his protests, which makes my head a bit swirly.

"You don't remember? You passed out at the pack house, you've been out for two hours..."

His words seem to trigger my memory, how I had a sudden onslaught of dizziness before my vision went black...I don't even remember hitting the ground...

"Fleura! You're awake! Are you alright?" A loud voice calls to me, and I look up to see Jessica coming through the door. She goes around Dakota to give me a fierce hug, and I sigh in relief after she lets me go...the girl is strong, I'll give her that.

"I'm fine...my head just hurts..." I answer.

"I bet it does, you hit it pretty hard when you fell to the floor." She says, and I wince again as the throbbing returns with a vengeance.

"Where does it hurt Flower?" Dakota murmurs.

"My temples..." I whimper, and he immediately places his hands on my temples, massaging them gently in circular motions...not only does his actions and touch alleviate the pain, but it feels really good...making my cheeks flush red with embarrassment as I try to remember we have an audience.

"Better?" He murmurs, and I nod shyly.

"You two are just the cutest couple!" Jess giggles, and my face reddens even more.

"Jessica, please stop embarrassing my mate...that's my job." Dakota chuckles, and I barely resist the urge to hide my face in his chest.

"My apologies Dakota, I forgot how much you enjoy doing that." She giggles, and I pout a little at my mates satisfied grin.

"As adorable as you look Flower, don't pout...you know I love you." He murmurs, his brown eyes staring deeply into mine as our foreheads touch....my heart racing at his words. I already know that he does...he's just never said it directly...

Then again...neither have I...

"You're always teasing me..." I mumble, "But I love you too..."

A purr rumbles in his chest as he smiles down at me, sparks dancing across my face as he cups my cheek...

"Awwww!!"Jess squeals excitedly, startling us from our moment. I had honestly forgotten she was here...

"Sorry, you guys are so affectionate...I'm honestly surprised you two aren't expecting more little sweethearts like Noah." She swoons, and my eyes widen.

"Noah...where's Noah?" I ask worriedly, my anxiety rearing it's ugly head as I realize that he was there when I fainted.

"It's okay Flower, he's spending time with his grandpa, they'll be here soon." He reassures, and a few seconds later the sounds of tiny feet comes running towards the door, and I look to see my baby running through it with a big smile on his face.

"Mommy!" He calls excitedly, only stopping so Dakota can lift him up to me. I pull him into my lap, and he wraps his arms around me as best as he can with his little arms.

"You feel better now?" He asks, his brown eyes gazing up me with worry.

"I do, thank you sweetie." I reply, ruffling the curls on his head.

"He was worried about you bunny, so were we."

I look up to see my Dad and Kelly standing in the doorway, and I smile at them.

"I'm fine now, don't worry." I reassure.

"What exactly happened?" Jessica asks, and I narrow my eyes.

"I don't know...I was feeling really hot, and when I got up to get some more tea I suddenly got really dizzy...the last thing I really remember was glass breaking before I blacked out." I answer, and Dakota worriedly pushes my hair back to check for any injuries...which I don't have. He's been very protective these last couple of weeks...more so than usual.

"Hopefully the doctor can give us some answers..." Dakota murmurs, and on cue the doctor actually comes in.

"I believe I can, Gamma Dakota." She says with a surprisingly happy tone, her dark hair pulled back to expose her blue eyes sparkling with excitement.

"What's going on with my mate Dr. Sandra?"

"Relax Gamma, it's good news." She chuckles, walking up to me to check my eyes with her light, and then my forehead for a fever.

"It is?" He tilts his head in confusion, which is quite cute.

"Well, yes. The test results came back for your blood work and other tests, and from what I can tell Fleura has caught the stomach bug that's been going around the pack lately...which isn't surprising considering your condition Miss Fleura, it should pass in a few days or so."

I pause at the last part, my mind going from all the kids I've been around lately on Noah's play dates...to 'my condition'.

"What do you mean, 'my condition'?" I ask, a little confused and anxious., and she gives me a equally confused look.

"Well, the stomach flu is common among expecting mothers...even she wolves get it from time to time." She explains...but my thoughts screech to halt again before I hear everything she says...

Expecting mothers?...does she...am I...

"Did you not know that you're pregnant?" She asks, and I can't seem to make words come out of my mouth...and it seems like no one else can either, for the room is completely silent...and Dakota is almost like a statue standing next to me.

"Oh. My. Goddess..." Jess murmurs in stunned awe, and I barely have enough time to brace myself when I see her ecstatic grin split across her face.

"You're pregnant!" She squeals, bouncing up and down like a spring loaded kangaroo. But I'm too distracted by Dakota's face appearing in front of me again to pay attention...his brown eyes are filled with surprise and excitement, his expression softer than I've ever seen it before.

"You're pregnant Flower...with our pup..." He murmurs almost like he's in a daze, his hands cradling my face carefully as he presses a soft kiss to my forehead. His content purring growing louder as he rests one of his hands down on my stomach...where I notice Noah stare up at us curiously, I shake myself into reality again as I pat his head.

"You're going to be a big brother Noah, isn't that exciting?" I ask , and his face scrunches up. I recognize that expression immediately, and pull his gaze back to mine.

"I promise you sweetie, you having a younger brother or sister will not change how much me and daddy love you...okay?" I murmur, and he nods after a moment.

"I'm going to be a grandpa again..." Dad murmurs, his smile radiant.

"And my mother is going to be thrilled..." Dakota chuckles, and I look down at my belly and place a hand there...excitement and nervousness flitting through my swirling thoughts...me and Dakota are having a baby...

"I can't believe it! Me, Amy and you are all going to have pups around the same time!" Jess squeals again...

And just when I recovered from the first round of shock, here comes another. Luckily, my mate isn't as lost for words this time.

"Are you serious?"

"Of course, I'm almost a month and a half...Amy's about a month, and maybe three weeks for you Fleura?"

I do the math, and nod after I realize she's right.

"Me and Amy were planning to tell everyone once our mates returned from their meeting today, but now we have even more great news to share!" She exclaims, and I sigh as Dakota curls his arms around me and Noah...and our combined thoughts are focused on our growing family.

~~~~~~~~(A month later)

"What are you doing Dakota?" I giggle as I slowly shuffle my feet in the direction he's guiding me, his hands securely over my closed eyes as he walks behind me. I know he's got a surprise of some kind, and that he's spent a good portion of the day keeping me away from upstairs...but I'm honestly not sure.

"Just a couple more steps flower, I promise that you'll love it!" He laughs excitedly, I can almost feel his wolf wagging happily in his head...

Whatever this is, it must be amazing.

"All right, I followed your exact instructions...and I think it's perfect." He murmurs as he pulls his hands away, and I stare in wide eyed shock as I take in the sight in front of me.

He finished the nursery...just like I wanted it, and it's perfect.

Dark purple now colors the once white walls, a perfect contrast to the light gray carpet. The black baby furniture we received from our shower is fully assembled and set up it the exact places I told him I wanted them to be...along with the rocking chair that dad made for me, with the blanket Dakota's mother made for the baby sitting in it.

A beautiful dream catcher mobile hangs over the crib, and I hold a hand over my mouth as I play with the black and white feathers before looking back at my incredible mate...his expression hesitant.

"Did you make this?" I ask as I play with the mobile, and he smiles.

"I started on it shortly after we found out, I just couldn't finish it before the shower...it was a bit stubborn-"

I cut him off as I walk towards him and press my lips to his, standing up on my tiptoes as both our height differences and my now showing belly interfere.

"I take it that you like it?" He chuckles.

"More than like, I love it...everything...the mobile, the room, and you..." I trail off as I kiss him again. "It's perfect...thank you..." I murmur, my eyes getting watery at how sweet my mate is.

"You're welcome Flower, I'm glad you love it...I wanted it to be just how you wanted it." He purrs, and I chuckle at the sight of purple paint on his face...a cute reminder of the room we painted together...which was followed by the events that got me pregnant.

He definitely notices my blush...and my distracting thoughts, because his eyes darken with a bit of hunger.

"I like the way you think Flower..." He purrs again, pulling me in for another kiss...this one a little deeper than the last. I close my eyes to enjoy the moment...

Then Dakota's phone rings.

"I swear to the goddess if it's Jake asking about baby names again, I'm gonna kill him..." He grumbles irritably as he answers, and I take advantage of his distraction to press kisses against his neck and shoulder...and I can tell from the way he shivers and purrs that he likes it.

~He loves how bold we've gotten dear, it excites him...~ My wolf growls lowly, and so does Dakota when I playfully nip his Adam's apple.

"I'll talk to you later Jake." He murmurs, hanging up before he pulls me back in for another kiss, his soft growls filling the room.

"You little minx..." He rumbles against my mouth before moving down my neck, and I grin.

"I know why you tease me now...it's fun." I murmur, then shiver as he starts working on the mark he gave me.

"It is...but I'm curious flower, what exactly do you have in mind that requires asking the Alpha about time off the pack land?"

I remember what I was going to discuss with him today, before I got distracted by Dakota's surprise. I pull back to see Dakota staring at me curiously, and sigh.

"I talked to my Dad yesterday...and we had a discussion about going up to the pack in Iowa for a visit, his parents...my grandparents, want to see me...and honestly I want to see them too...my memories of them are vague.

I figured we could make it a family trip, and Noah could meet his great grandparents..."

I trail off, but before I can speak again Dakota presses a finger to my lips.

"You don't have to talk me into it Sihu, it sounds like a great idea." He smiles, and I can feel mine spreading across my face.

"Really?"

"Of course, I want to meet the rest of your family too...and I'm sure Noah is going to love more grandparents to spoil him rotten." He chuckles, and I hug him tightly.

How did I ever get so lucky?

~~EIGHTEEN~~

Dakota

I smile as I look down at my mate and pup, both of them out cold as we fly to Iowa. Fleura's head rests on my shoulder as she softly snores, while my son rests his on her belly, her arm curled around him to help hold him on her lap as he holds on to the stuffed turtle she gave him.

So cute...

I press a kiss to the top of Fleura's head, purring softly as she nuzzles into my shoulder. She's slept most of the way here, as well as Noah despite both of them being excited about their first plane flight...after taking off and the first few minutes of being in the air, they were out like lights...which considering the fact that they both were up early out of their excitement, I'm not surprised.

Unfortunately though, the announcement to fasten seat belts and prepare for landing signifies that our one hour flight is over, and it's time for them to wake up.

"Flower...Flower, time to get up baby." I murmur as I brush her face, and after a couple of attempts her eyes finally flutter open.

"Dakota?" She mumbles drowsily, and I smile.

"We're about to land, time for you and Noah to buckle up." I explain, and as she sits up she tightens her hold on our pup, stifling a yawn before reaching down to ruffle his blonde curls.

"Noah, wake up sweetie." She murmurs, and he yawns before looking up at her with sleepy brown eyes.

"Are we there yet?" He mumbles, an we chuckle.

"Almost little man, you gotta buckle up though...the planes about to land." I respond, and he nods as he gets back in his seat, Fleura helping buckle him in before she buckles in herself...a little bit difficult considering how much our other pup has grown.

She wraps her hand in mine, her other resting on top of her belly.

~She looks so beautiful carrying our pup...~ Zayev rumbles happily, and I have to agree.

~She certainly does...~

~We are very lucky...the goddess gave us the perfect mate...~ He continues.

~Definitely...~

She looks up at me, a curious look on her face.

"What is it, Dakota?" She questions, and I just smile and lift her hand up to my mouth to kiss the back of it.

"Nothing Sihu, just thinking about you." I reply, taking great joy in how she blushes. I love how she's gotten bolder, but her bashful moments are something I'll always adore.

After a few more minutes the plane finally starts to descend, and I can tell by the look on their faces that Fleura enjoyed touching down less than Noah, his little cry of delight getting some chuckles from the other passengers...while I'm sure in my mates case it just unsettled her stomach.

"You alright baby?" I ask, and she nods with some hesitation.

"I'm fine, I think I prefer take off more than touch down..." She murmurs, and I squeeze her hand.

"Do you need to go to the bathroom after we get off the plane?"

She shakes he head. "I'm fine, I promise." She assures.

After we finally exit the plane, we grab our bags and head to the parking area...finding our rental car waiting for us in the lot. We load our bags in and put Noah in his car seat before we start on our way towards the Lunar Falls pack...the home of my mates family.

I can sense her nervousness through our link, her mind racing at the anticipation of seeing her grandparents again for the first time since she was a little girl...and I take her hand in mine once more.

"Relax Flower...they already love you, the fact that you're an adult now will never change that." Her tense expression relaxes, a soft smile spreading across her face.

"Thank you Ohpitsa....I needed to hear that."

"Of course Flower, anytime."

We continue on to the pack in silence, and as we cross into the territory I take in a flurry of excitement...no doubt the pack has been anticipating her arrival, and I smile.

This is going to be even more interesting than I thought it would be...

Fleura

I've never felt so exhilarated...and so exhausted at the same time.

My heart and mind seems to be overflowing with love these days, even more so after meeting my grandparents again and introducing them to my family...after the initial reactions of happy tears, they began dotting over both Noah and me just like my father and my mate, Noah already calling them pawpaw and Nana...which only added to their joy at seeing they would have another great grandchild soon.

We spent some time looking through the albums my grandmother made, pictures of me from birth to toddler...pictures that included my mother, which help me finally realize how right they are when anyone says I look just like her....and helped bring back even more memories.

My Aunt, Dad's sister, and her mate came here too, along with her four children...my cousins, along with their mates and children...I've learned so many names and faces since I first arrived that I'm honestly surprised I can remember them all...

And it wasn't just my biological family that swarmed around me, but other pack members too...a good portion of which grieved over me and my mother after our death was confirmed...it was hard to believe that so many people mourned me...considering most barely knew me at all back then...but I that's how packs work...whether you're blood or not, a pack is family.

There have been so many people coming up to us in our time here, talking to me and hugging me...some of them crying, all them happy to see me. Though...Dakota has had a difficult time with it, his territorial daddy behavior has been on a record high, I've lost count of how many times his wrapped his around my belly and growled possessively...grumbling 'mine' anytime an unrelated male comes anywhere near me...as cute as it is, I still scold him a little...none of those males were flirting with me in the slightest.

After spending a few days in Lunar Falls, I finally got the courage to ask about something important I wanted to do before I went home...

Visit my mothers grave.

It's where I'm at now, the pack cemetery not too far from the pack house for me to walk...so while Dakota and Noah are visiting with my brother, I follow the stone path that leads to it by myself as the cold fall air blows through my hair....it doesn't take me long to find my mothers, for she is laid to rest where all the other Alpha's and Luna's are.

I stare at her headstone for a moment, my eyes tracing over the words carved in stone.

Saraphina Nash Anderson

A Loving Luna, Mate, and Mother...

I swallow hard as my eyes begin to water, lowering myself to sit on the stone bench in front of her grave, I let out a shakey breath as I try to think of all the thing I wanted to say to her...

"I wish I could have come to see you sooner Mama, but as you use to tell me, life has peculiar way of changing people's plans..." I start, looking down at the bouquet of daffodils I'm holding...they were the flowers that used to pick for her, the wild growing ones anyway, which of course made them her favorite.

"I certainly didn't plan on losing you so soon...or forgetting who you were for all this time." I continue, the tears spilling over my cheeks.

"There's so much you never got to see...me growing up, my first shift, finding my mate...Noah, the pup I'm carrying now..." I hiccup as I wipe my eyes, my vision blurry.

"I know from dad and my returning memories that you loved me....but I just wish that I had the chance to tell you in person how much I loved you...to know for certain that you knew that...I guess that's the biggest reason I came here today..."

I bow my head as I lose the ability to speak, my tears dripping onto the flowers I'm holding. However, I jerk my head up as I feel something touch my cheeks...unusually warm compared to the cold air around me...and my eyes widen in disbelief at the sight in front of me...

Mother...her transparent form standing in front of me, her smile just as as gentle as her hands cupping my cheeks...

I open my mouth to speak, to say anything, but nothing comes out...and I watch as she leans forward to press a kiss to my forehead like she used to...and as the warmth spreads across my forehead, she disappears...the sound of someone calling me snapping me back to the present.

"Mama!"

I look over my shoulder to see both Dakota and Noah coming towards me, and I turn back for a split second as I try to make sense of what just happened...

~She knows child...that's all that matters...~ Aurora whispers, and I smile as I look down to see my little boy at my feet, reaching up to me while clutching onto something.

"Hey baby, what do you got there?" I ask, and he gazes up at me with concern as he places the item in my hand, a macaroni necklace...

"You made this for me? Thank you baby..."

"Why are you crying Mama?" He asks, and I immediately wipe off my cheeks with my long sleeves.

"I was just a little sad, but I'm okay now..." I answer, and he grabs onto my hand with his little one.

"Don't be sad...you got me..." He replies, my eyes watering again.

"And me too, Sihu." Dakota murmurs as he sits down next to me, and I lean into his side as he curls his arm around me, Noah crawling into his lap with some assistance.

"You're right...I've got both of my sweet boys with me..." I murmur, and we sit together long enough to watch the sun begin to sink, casting a beautiful array of colors in the sky...my heart feeling lighter than it ever has.

~~NINETEEN~~

"Noah!? Noah baby!?" I call out frantically as I move as quickly as possible through the racks full of clothing, my heart racing almost as fast as my thoughts. I had only taken my eyes off of him for a second, but when I turned back around he was nowhere in sight...and right now it's all I can do not to have a total panic attack.

"Noah?" I call again, ignoring people's looks as my flats tap against the concrete floor.

"Mommy!" I hear him exclaim, and I turn around to see him sitting on the shoulders of one of the store employees, the boy looking about eighteen.

"Oh goddess, there you are baby!" I sigh in relief as I walk to them, and the boy smiles as he hands Noah to me.

"I found him wandering around in the toy department, I figured he was looking for you too." He chuckles, and I notice his name tag says Jason.

"Thank you so much, he usually doesn't wander off like this." I say as I hold Noah on my hip, and Jason nods.

"It's quite alright, he's a real sweet kid. Have a good day ma'am." He says as he walks away, and I look down at the pup in my arms...his sad, puppy dog expression admittedly cute.

"Sweetheart, you really scared me baby...didn't I tell you not to wander off by yourself?" I say as I ruffle his curls.

"Sorry mommy..."

"It's alright baby, just don't do it again. What were you even doing so far away?" I say as I start walking back to my previous place in the store.

"I saw this...for baby." He answers, holding up a cute animal plushie in his hand, and I smile as I take it.

"You picked this out for the baby?" I ask, finding the soft elephant very cute. He nods, putting his hand on my belly.

"We can play together!" He smiles brightly, and I kiss his forehead.

"So sweet, you're a great big brother."

He giggles as we continue back to our former activity, which consists of shopping for his little sibling. Me, Jess, and Amy are all out shopping today, after their insistence that I was spending too much time in the house. I was a little hesitant at first, not really comfortable with going to town when I'm so close to being due...I know I still have a couple of weeks, but Dr. Sandra said it was entirely possible for pups to come early, though considering this is my first pregnancy it's not as likely.

Both Jess and Amy have already welcomed their little ones into the world, which isn't surprising considering they were both further along than I was. Jessica and Jacob now have a beautiful baby girl named Vivian, who at a little over a month old already has her daddy wrapped tightly around her little fingers. As for Amy and Paul, they have an adorable little boy named Mason...whose literally the mini version of his daddy...

Which is why I was so surprised they wanted to do a girls outing, being that they recently had their pups. But Jess explained that Jacob is fully capable of taking care of Vivian for a few hours, and can handle diaper duty and bottle feeding if necessary...just as Paul is capable of doing so with Mason while we spend some time together.

We had decided to go shopping for necessities for the baby, like onesies, diapers, pacifiers and things like that...especially diapers, we're going to need plenty of those now. The only reason we didn't really have too much of that with Noah is because he had started potty training by the time we adopted him.

Anyway, when I realized that Noah had wandered off, we all split up to look for him...now that I've found him though, we can regroup.

~I found him girls, let's meet back at the baby clothes before we go for lunch.~ I send through the link, and after they all answer and agree, saying they be here in a few minutes. I continue on to the clothing, remembering that I saw a little outfit I just adored...and would match Noah's pick perfectly.

"What do you think of this one baby? It matches your elephant." I say as I hold up the one I liked, and he nods eagerly.

"It's pretty mommy!"

"I think so too." I giggle, and I quickly make my way up to the register with my basket, paying for everything before I go back to wait for the girls, only to have Noah pull on the hem of my peach colored cardigan anxiously as he walks beside me.

"What is it baby? Is something wrong?" I ask, and I look down to see he's staring at something behind me.

"Why is that angry lady following us?" He asks, and I immediately turn around to see a face I never wanted to see again.

Cassie. Dakota's ex.

"Get behind me baby." I murmur, not liking the fury in her eyes one bit. He goes behind me without a word, his hands clutching my jeans.

"What do you want Cassie?" I ask tersely, I may still feel a little intimidated by her hostility, but I'll be damned if she directs it anywhere near my pup.

She glares angrily at my pregnant belly, and I instinctively curl an arm around it.

"You...you took him away from me. You got in the way, and now you're carrying his pup!" She growls, stepping towards me. I let out a growl of my own, flashing my canines at her threateningly. She falters a bit in her path as she locks eyes with me, no doubt my wolf's gold irises are glowing as she rises to the surface.

"You going to act brave now little brat?" She sneers, and as she moves closer my hand curls into a fist...the second she's two feet from me, I'm making sure she doesn't get closer.

"Leave mommy alone!" Noah's voice calls out angrily, and before I can stop him he darts in between me and Cassie, and to my absolute shock he kicks her square in the shin, hard.

"You little shit!" She snarls, and the second she glares down at him I act on instinct.

"You keep your hands off of my son!" I growl at her, pushing her back, and just as she grabs my wrists two pairs of strong arms grab her from behind, and I recognize the faces of the two warriors Dakota and the guys gave us for protection detail.

"Remove your hands from Gamma Fleura immediately!" They order, and as I try to pull away from her strong grip she struggles.

"Let her go!"

She finally releases her grip, which sends me stumbling back into a concrete support column, and I gasp as both my back and head against it...a sharp pain shooting through both.

"Fleura! Fleura? Are you okay?"

I look up to see Jess and Amy in front of me, another warrior standing behind them, I try to straighten up only feel another shock of pain....this time in my lower abdomen.

"Fleura!" They call again, and I whimper.

"Mommy?" Noah calls, and the fear that courses through me turns my body cold.

"Something's wrong...I..." I stumble for words, and they immediately come to my side.

"We're taking you to the hospital, now. Call Gamma Dakota, tell him everything!" Jess barks in her Luna tone, and everyone starts moving. Amy picks up Noah in her arms as Jess holds onto me, trying to help me move as quick as I can manage through the pain.

"It's going to be okay Fleura, I promise."

Dakota

I burst through the hospital doors at dead sprint, my heart racing as Flower's panic screams in my head. Mine is filled with fear, confusion, dread...and anger...more like fury.

Cassie....that damn woman attacked my pregnant mate in front of my son, and now she's in the hospital. I want to deal with that wretched woman myself...but Fleura is far more important, she's scared to death and in pain...she needs me right now.

"Dakota! Slow down!" Jake and Paul call out to me, moving slower as they carry their pups in their carrier seats. But I keep moving.

"Dakota, over here." I glance up to see Jess waving at me, and immediately join her and Amy in the small waiting area.

"Where is she?" I ask urgently, and Jessica grabs hold of me to stop me from pacing.

"You need to calm down, now...Fleura needs you calm, not panicked." She states.

"I need to find her, she's scared-"

"And so is your son." She interrupts, and I peer behind her to see Noah sitting on the couch, half dried tears on his cheeks as he stares blankly at a stuffed elephant in his hands. I instantly calm down some, realizing just how scared and confused he probably is right now...

I take a deep breath and walk towards him slowly, crouching down to meet his gaze.

"Hey buddy, look at me." I say softly, my wolf whining at the sight of his watery eyes.

"Everything is going to be okay, I promise." I reassure, and he sniffles.

"Bad lady hurt mommy...I tried to stop her...but..." He whimpers, and gently pull him in for a hug.

"It's not your fault buddy, you did your best to protect mommy, and I'm proud of you for that." I murmur, rubbing the back of his head as his tears dampen my shirt.

"It's not your fault, okay?" I repeat as I look down at him, and he nods as I wipe his eyes. Noticing the stuffed animal again, I smile, its brand new...which means...

"You picked that out for the baby, didn't you?" I ask, and he nods.

"Then you hold onto that for me while I check on mommy, then when the baby's here you can give it to them...sound good?"

He nods, and I stand after I kiss the top of his head. As I do a doctor walks in, and I can smell that she's a werewolf.

"I'm Fleura's mate, what's going on?" I talk softly, and she sighs.

"Your mate has gone into early labor, which isn't a problem considering the baby is developed enough. The problem is that the child is breech, and we can't get them to turn." She explains, and I swallow hard.

"Breech? What does that mean?" I ask.

"It means that instead of facing head down like they're supposed to, the pup is in the wrong position for a natural birth...and we can't get the pup to turn to the right direction. We're already prepared to do a c-section, but you're mate is very stressed and is having difficulty calming down."

"Then let me go back there, if there's anyone that can calm her down it's me." I reply, and after a moment of deliberation she nods, and I follow her to the room...only stopping to change into scrubs and wash my hands.

The second I enter the room I go to my mate, her pained face covered in sweat.

"Flower, Flower, look at me...look at me." I plead, and she turns her gaze to me, her eyes filled with panic.

"Dakota...I'm scared..."

"I know, but it's okay...I'm right here. Just take deep breaths...come on.." I murmur, and after a moment of doing that she settles down a little.

"Our baby is okay sweetheart, they're just not in the right position...because they're stubborn like their daddy." I murmur, and she almost smiles.

"So they're going to do a c-section to deliver them, and I promise I'll be right here the whole time."

She nods, and I press my forehead to hers.

"Let's meet our pup."

~~~~~~~

About two hours later I walk out to the waiting room, now filled with both Fleura's family and mine. Hers no doubt booked the first flight here the second they were called. My mother and sisters are here too, and they all look up to me anxiously as I enter the room.

"Dakota, what is it?"Jessica and my mother ask at once, and I can't stop the smile from splitting my face.

"It's a boy!" I announce, and the room erupts with cheers as I'm engulfed in a hug by my mother.

"Fleura's still a bit tired, but you guys can come in for a visit." I say, and then crouch down so I can pick up Noah.

"What do you say little man? Wanna see your little brother?" I ask, and he nods as he holds on tight to the plushie.

I lead everyone to the room, opening the door to see my beautiful mate holding our new pup, her tired smile a beautiful sight. Everyone files in quietly, not wanting to disturb the now quiet pup, and I bring Noah to see him first, his wide eyes filled with curiosity.

"Noah, everyone, I would like you to meet Kova Jackson." I introduce, and Mom's eyes widen.

"After your father?" She murmurs, and both me and Fleura nod. Noah reaches an empty hand towards him, and Kova grabs it tightly.

"He looks just like you baby." Mom sighs, and I turn to give Fleura a smile, which she returns as she touches her forehead to mine.

"Welcome to the family Kova."

~~TWENTY~~

Fleura

So precious...

I stare at my boys quietly after taking their picture with my phone, a smile on my face as I take in the sight of all of them sleeping soundly in the recliner. My mate snoring softly as he cradles Kova to his chest, our now two month pup clutching both my mates long braid and a handful of his shirt, drooling a bit. Noah snuggles up on his lap, still in his solar system pajamas and holding on to his stuffed turtle.

~Our boys, I love the sound of that.~ Aurora purrs happily, and I have to agree.

I quietly walk towards them, leaning down to kiss Dakota's forehead...and he immediately stops snoring.

"I know you're awake Ohpitsa, it's time to get up..." I whisper in his ear, and he opens his eyes as he smiles...those beautiful brown irises full of sleepy mischief.

"Good morning Flower." He murmurs, his free hand reaching to cup my cheek as I lean down to kiss his lips like he wants...his morning kiss a requirement before he gets up.

"Good morning, did I miss something last night?" I ask, looking down at our pups, and he chuckles.

"Kova started crying at around 6 this morning, so I got up to keep him from waking you...and Noah woke up too. I planned on staying down here until he settled, but I guess we all fell asleep down here." He whispers, and Noah stirs a little.

"Well, it's eleven thirty now, so I think it's time for everyone to wake up...except maybe Kova, he can sleep if it keeps him calm." I murmur, and he smiles as he notices my dress, the rose pink wrap dress not a normal part of my morning attire...neither is the light make up, heels, or pinned back hair.

"Well, don't you look gorgeous." He murmurs, and I blush.

"Thank you, I figured I'd dress up today." I reply as I pick up Noah and prop him on my hip, looking a little groggy as his eyes blink open.

"What's the special occasion Flower?" He asks as he stands up, and I'm completely shocked...has he forgotten what today is?

"You don't remember?" I question, and his eyes narrow in concentration, trying to figure out what I'm talking about.

"No...it's something important, isn't it?" He replies, looking a bit sheepish.

"I'd say it is." I chuckle, and Noah looks up to me as I tap him on the nose. "Can you tell daddy what mommy told you last night at bedtime?" I ask, and he smiles.

"Happy Birthday Daddy!!!" Noah exclaims, making Kova stir as Dakota's eyes widen in shock.

"Goddess, today's really the 5th of December?" He says, and I nod.

"Yes, how on earth did you forget?"

"I don't know, I guess I got consumed with the pups..." He murmurs.

"Well Birthday boy, how about you go get dressed, and then we can go out for your birthday. And since Jess agreed to look after the boys, we can have some time to ourselves..." I reply, and as he leans down to peck me on the lips, we both make a sudden discovery.

"I think before I do that, I'll change Kova's diaper first." He says with a crinkled up face, mine looking the same no doubt. Occasionally, having heightened senses is more of a bad thing than good.

We all head upstairs together, and while Dakota handles little Kova, I help Noah get dressed, changing out his pajamas for a pair of khaki pants and his favorite superman shirt.

"You still got daddy's present hidden baby?" I ask as I slip on his shoes, and he bobs his head excitedly as he gets up, running over to pull the card he made out from under the giant teddy bear sitting in the corner of the room.

"Perfect, now hang onto that." I say as I scoop him back up in my arms, running a brush through his wild curls before going to the baby's room...and I smile happily at what I see.

Kova, in a fresh diaper, laying on his back on the changing table as my mate hovers over him, playfully blowing raspberries on Kova's belly...our little boy smiling and making cute gurgling noises in response.

"Are my boys having fun?" I giggle as I watch, adoring just how playful and sweet Dakota is...

"Oh yeah, peanut and I are trying to play the laughing game, he loves it." He chuckles as he plays with Kova's kicking feet, the little boy still making those gurgling sounds as he smiles.

"As adorable it is, you need to go get ready...I'll finish with Kova." I reply, and Dakota pouts playfully before he leaves the room, kissing my cheek on the way out. After sitting down Noah in the rocking chair, I hunt for a onesie that'll actually fit Kova these days, he's grown so much in two months it's been difficult to keep up with his spurts.

"Alright you cute little roly-poly, let's see if this one will fit you." I murmur as I pull out one that looks like a little tux, and I sigh in relief as it does, and he looks adorable.

"What a handsome little man, now for your socks!" I put his little gray socks, hoping that he manages not to lose them before we get to the pack house, goddess knows he's got a thing against them...

"Goddess, if you keep growing this fast, you're going to be as tall as your daddy..." I say to him, and I hear a chuckle from the hallway.

"A very good possibility, I was the tallest kid in my third grade class, and the Jackson genes run strong." Dakota says proudly as he scoops Kova up, my mate now changed into a black dress shirt and jeans, the long sleeves of the shirt pushed up to his elbows and the first few buttons left open as his Gamma pendant lays on top. He looks very handsome, I've never seen him this dressed up before...

"I'm glad you like it Flower, I figured you would." He chuckles, no doubt reading my thoughts...and my face tinges pink in embarrassment. How is it that even after having his child, I can still get bashful like this over the simple things?

We grab our things and head out to his truck, and I can feel my budding excitement as we buckle the boys into their seats and drive up to the pack house, knowing something that I've been keeping a secret from Dakota for the past couple of weeks...which isn't an easy thing to do....so I pray to the goddess that he doesn't know already.

Once we arrive at the pack house, we all walk in, the place unusually quiet...and I nearly fill it with a laugh.

"Where is everyone? Usually the pack house is loud and bustling." Dakota says, and I bite my lip to suppress my excitement.

I suggest we check the dining room, and the second we walk in the lights turn on.

"Surprise!!!"

Dakota's eyes widen in shock as he takes in the sight of the party, our family and friends filling the room along with the decorations and food, a banner with 'Happy Birthday Dakota!' hangs on the back wall, and a small table full of presents sits under it.

"Happy Birthday Ohpitsa." I murmur, and he turns to me with surprise.

"You planned this, Flower?" He asks with awestruck eyes, and I nod.

"It's your first birthday since we met, I wanted to make it special." I reply, and my face reddens as he pulls me in for a kiss in front of everyone, a little embarrassed at the whistling and clapping.

"Oh Sihu, you've already made it special...you've given me more than I ever dreamed of." He murmurs, his soft purr bringing back those butterflies in my stomach...

I hope I never lose them...ever.

~~~~~

After spending time eating and laughing, and enjoying his birthday cake after blowing out the candles, we move onto presents...and after both the sentimental from the family, and the gag gifts from Jake and Paul that got us all laughing hysterically...it was almost time for the party to end...but Dakota wanted to say something first.

"I have to thank everybody for coming, and admit that I never expected all this today...you guys, and my lovely mate helped make this day memorable in all the best ways." He starts, and I blush again as he gives me that adoring look.

"But, before we all go, there's something else that I want to do right here..."

I turn around to hand Kova to Dakota's mother, and the expression of shock on her face concerns me. Tilting my head in confusion, I hear other people gasp.

"Flower, there's one more present I want for my birthday." He calls to me, and I turn back around to face Dakota, only stare at him in complete shock as he drops down on one knee.

"Fleura Anderson, you have brought me so much joy since you first came into my life. You've given me so much love, and so much to love with our little boys...I want nothing more than to keep that love growing as our family does..."

My eyes water as he pulls out a box from his pocket, my hands shaking as I hold them over my mouth.

"So Flower, would you give me the greatest present of all by marrying me?" He says, opening the box to reveal a beautiful ring.

I'm completely speechless for a second, struggling to remember how to breathe.

~This is the part where you say yes sweetheart...~ Aurora murmurs, and I snap out of it just enough to answer, tears spilling over my cheeks.

"Yes..." I reply shakily, and everyone cheers as Dakota slide the ring on my finger, a humongous smile on his face as he pulls me in for a kiss, my heart racing a mile a minute.

I don't think I've ever been this happy before in my life, and I have a feeling it's only going to be better...

~~EPILOGUE~~

~Eight years later~

The Goddess has really blessed me and Dakota, that's for certain. Our house is now filled with the laughter and little thumping feet of pups, six of them in total.

Little Noah isn't so little anymore, at ten years old he's really grown up...and even though he no longer desires to be held, he still sticks to me like glue as much as he can...a mama's boy through and through. He's already starting to show that he'll be taller than me by the time he's in ninth grade, shooting up like a bean pole. His blonde curls have only gotten wilder and longer, and he's very adamant about keeping them that way.

Kova has also shot up, and from the looks of it he'll be even taller than Noah...just like Dakota predicted. Kova is pretty much a miniature version of his daddy with his black hair and brown eyes, especially since he's decided to let his hair grow long instead of letting me cut it, wanting it to be just like his dad.

Our third is a little girl we named Narah, Dakota's first baby girl. Much to my delight, she favors both of us equally, and to my mates delight she developed heterochromia like me...with one blue, and one brown eye. Her brunette curls kept shoulder length the way she likes them, at seven years old she's already so assertive at strong willed...which makes me incredibly happy, and Dakota a little nervous.

Pups number four and five are our five year old fraternal twins Zane and Hiraya, who have proven just how strong Dakota's genes really are with their black hair and dads skin tone, though we were surprised yet again by my eyes showing up again in both of them. Zane having blue and hazel, while Hiraya's are brown and green...it quite the phenomenon, but we don't question it it too much...especially since Hiraya is showing signs of having the same ability as me and my mother, retrocognition...the ability to see the past.

And finally, our last pup Citlali, true princess of the family at two years old. To be truthful, me and Dakota had planned on making the twins the last pups, but much to our surprise, she became our unexpected final addition....and I have to admit she's the cutest surprise. Out of all of our biological pups, she favors me the most, her dirty blonde hair and complexion may be darker than mine...but she still helps me and Noah fit in a little more, especially with those blues eyes to go with it.

After bringing her into the family, me and Dakota have both made sure to always use protection...because as much as I love all of our beautiful pups, our house is officially full, we don't have any more room...and frankly, after two c-sections and three natural deliveries...I'm done having pups. Dakota didn't argue, both because he knows better, and he has the big family he dreamed of...it's certainly bigger than Jake or Paul's with them only having three pups each.

Speaking of which, Dakota and Noah are visiting the pack house today, part of their father son time. The rest of the pups are with me, all of them sitting with me in the living room watching their favorite show- Loony

Tunes, giggling at the antics of Buggs Bunny and Daffy Duck. Citlali sits in my lap with her sippy cup, while Narah and Kova cuddle on either side of me, and the twins sit on the floor propped up on pillows...the only thing that could make this better is if my other two boys were here.

"Mama!"

I turn to the open door to see Noah running in, my mate following behind him with a happy smile on his face.

"Daddy!" Our other pups cry out, swarming him as he crouches down to their level. Citlali remains in my lap though, she's inherited my more bashful demeanor, so she just bounces happily as he comes towards us, Noah sitting beside me first.

"Goddess, I love this greeting." He chuckles as he kisses me, then Citlali, and then sits down on the couch, Noah happily between us. The rest of our pups crawl up on the couch, packing it full as Dakota puts his arm behind my head.

"How was your day Ohpitsa?" I ask, and he chuckles.

"It was pretty good, training was light, and I believe Noah here has himself a little girlfriend." He says, and Noah scowls adorably.

"Is that so? What girl is doting over our little man?" I ask as I ruffle Noah's hair.

"Vivian." Dakota chuckles, and I look at him in shock.

"Vivian? Jake's daughter?" I ask, and he nods.

"She keeps chasing and hugging me, and trying to kiss my cheek...she's weird!" Noah pouts, and me and Dakota share a knowing look.

"Well she likes you baby, she probably thinks you're cute." I murmur, and he huffs.

"She's still weird." He grumbles, and I suppress laughter.

~You think it's possible that, you know?~ I ask Dakota through our link, and he grins.

~It's a definite possibility, she's an alpha child after all...bonds can start showing at young ages, though we won't really know for sure until both of them are older and go through their first shift.~

I smile to myself, finding it absolutely sweet...and I know that despite his pouty behavior, he secretly likes her too.

"Well honey, I think it's cute..." I murmur, and Dakota chuckles.

"Mom..." He groans, and I smile as we all continue to watch together, the couch just as full as my heart. There is no other place rather be, surrounded by so much love...with my handsome mate and husband by my side, and our beautiful pups around us.

Who would've guessed that this all started with two lone wolves crossing each other's paths...and falling for each other?

www.ingramcontent.com/pod-product-compliance
Lightning Source LLC
Chambersburg PA
CBHW072159070526
44585CB00015B/1213